STRUCTURES
of
GRACE

STRUCTURES
of
GRACE

The Business Practices
of the Economy of Communion

John Gallagher and Jeanne Buckeye
With Forewords by Michael Naughton
and John Mundell

NEW CITY PRESS
of the Focolare
Hyde Park, NY

Published in the United States by New City Press
202 Comforter Blvd., Hyde Park, NY 12538
www.newcitypress.com
© 2014 John Gallagher and Jeanne Buckeye

Cover design by Leandro De Leon

A catalog record is available from the Library of Congress.

ISBN: 978–1–56548–551–8

Printed in the United States of America

To my wife, Pat, and to our children, grandchildren, and great-grandchildren; for these are the treasured relationships that form my own structure of grace.

John Gallagher

For Mom, Dad, Mary, Barbara and all my family, who have been wonderful teachers in the economy of love.

Jeanne Buckeye

Contents

Forewords... ix

Preface 1

Introduction.. 7

Chapter One
   Understanding the Economy of Communion........ 13

Characteristics of EoC Companies

Chapter Two
   Their Customers... 39

Chapter Three
   Competitive Practices and Pricing...................... 65

Chapter Four
   Business Processes and Work Design.................. 85

Chapter Five
   Employees and Hiring Practices 109

Chapter Six
   Organizational Culture and Leadership 135

Chapter Seven
   Their Defining Moments................................. 155

Chapter Eight
   Reflections and Conclusions 179

Appendix
   Research Methodology.................................... 193
   References 201

Index 205

Forewords

The last temptation is the greatest treason:
To do the right thing for the wrong reason.

T. S. Eliot, Murder in the Cathedral

John Gallagher and Jeanne Buckeye have given us a wonderful gift in this book. They have described, especially for an American audience, a business movement with deep cultural roots that is relatively unknown in the United States. While this movement in many respects is in an infancy stage, its importance cannot be underestimated. At the heart of the project is a radical claim, namely that people can grow spiritually and in union with others through the most basic and common practices of business. The claim, however, is not that business can do this by itself. Unlike other value-based business movements that emphasize corporate social responsibility, business ethics, corporate citizenship or social entrepreneurship, what Gallagher and Buckeye describe here is a movement deeply rooted in a cultural soil with rejuvenating spiritual sources. It is this connection between the culture and business that makes the movement so interesting and this book so important.

What you are about to read are stories of businesses created by men and women who believe that through daily work and the conduct of business one can truly *see* and *be* "Christ among us." As businesses of the Economy of Communion in Freedom (EOC), the dozen or so North American companies described here share a purpose and values with hundreds of other companies of the EOC operating around the world. Theirs is a great adventure: to create a community of businesses that express a spirituality of unity. In contrast to an economy dedicated to profit-seeking above all else, the economy to which these companies commit themselves is one that manages work and pursues profits as a means of expressing solidarity, especially with the poor, but also with co-workers, customers, suppliers, the community and even competitors. And although one may correctly assert that EOC businesses seek to do good, the owners of these businesses are not merely "do-gooders," in the philanthropic meaning of that term. To paraphrase the language of *Vocation of the Business Leader,* they have a vision of *being* good by offering goods that are truly good and services that truly serve. But they are also interested in doing well and, through prudent choices and good fortune, generating a profit. One might say that their interest is in doing the right thing for the right reason.

The co-authors' curiosity about this oddly named group—the Economy of Communion—began with their acquaintance with an EOC entrepreneur who accepted their request to write a business case about his engineering consulting business, Mundell & Associates. When John Mundell invited them to visit his business, conduct interviews and review organizational processes, they became interested in the terminology related to certain practices that was encouraged among EOC owners, e.g., to "see things together," to "humanize" the economy, to create a "communion of goods," and to "trust in Providence." For business professors trained to use the conventional language of management and economics to describe what they were seeing, this kind of language was intriguing. And so was the EOC experiment that used such terms to express deeply held values consistent with their approach to doing business. The Mundell experience prompted the authors to keep on digging. Are these EOC companies different? If so, what is different about them? Do they all operate like Mundell & Associates? What is it they have in common? Is it business practice or business philosophy—or both—that makes them "EOC?"

The research objective was to describe the business practices of EOC companies: not to analyze these practices, or to systematically compare them to other companies, or to categorize them according to the conventions of management language and studies. The result is more reportage and reflection than analysis or critique. Although readers of *Structures of Grace* will learn a lot about the individual companies that participated in this 18-month study, the focus is on the set of companies, not on discrete profiles of each firm and its owners, employees, customers, or practices. Reading the book one can imagine the authors discussing management concepts, then sitting down with a group of owners to hear what they all have to say on the subject. In reporting on these "conversations," the authors show significant restraint and respect, hesitating to draw overly broad conclusions, leaving open questions where owners have simply not said enough, acknowledging the voices of the smallest companies and the larger ones equally. They do occasionally venture into conclusions about something special or different in these companies. One of these conclusions—or insights—relates to the EOC approach to relationships and their apparent significance. And about this I want to say a word.

There is nothing new in businesses claiming to care about customers, or about cultivating and building on customer relationships, or about nuanced strategies that define "relationship management" as a key asset or managerial function. Increasingly we hear reports that the capacities and demands of social media are causing some businesses to rethink the emphasis on relationships because with Tweeting, instantaneous on-line reviews and blogging, customers seem to be less interested in "the business I know I can trust," than they are in the "best deal" or the best recommendation of recent users. This varies, no doubt, depending on the product or service. In any case, a primary reason for cultivating relationships in business has been the power of loyalty and the recommendations or references it engenders; this reasoning is, at heart, utilitarian. Relationships are cultivated for their potential impact on revenues and profits. But this is not the only way to think about the importance of relationships.

As my colleagues, friends and students know well, the line from T. S. Eliot's "Murder in the Cathedral" with which I opened this Foreword is a personal favorite. More than a reminder that motive always matters in human action, it also names the consequence of not doing "the right thing" in order to gain an advantage over someone who has reason or desire to trust us: treason. "To do the right thing for the wrong reason" in the realm of business relationships is to tend and nurture them only for their economic value. Even corporate philanthropy, which has every potential of being an authentic good, can be corrupted by utilitarian motives. To cultivate good will and good relationships through corporate giving "because it is good public relations," is, as Lynn Sharp Paine has suggested, to hint very broadly that this is no act of generosity, but a marketing strategy, one that can be quickly ended if the return is marginal. This, the EOC seems to be saying, is precisely the opposite of their motives in emphasizing relationships arising from a business encounter. They are instead responding to the most basic of Christian calls. To love one another. To be a gift to each other. To be the unity that Christ prayed for in his last hours. If the authors are correct in thinking that the EOC's preoccupation with relationships can be understood in this light, I can only say, bravo. If businesses were to adopt EOC practices in this regard, "humanizing the economy" would take on real meaning for the average person.

For the EOC companies in this study, managing relationships is not entirely—or even mostly—revenue driven. It is rooted in a central point in Christian theology that apparently animates the EOC vision itself. That is, Christ lives and lives among us. For the Christian, each encounter with another is a potential encounter with Christ. And reciprocally, each person we encounter may legitimately look for Christ in us. Therefore, each encounter becomes a moment in which to express or to find the love of Christ in the world. And each relationship is important because it carries within it an opportunity for the exchange of the gift that is the love of Christ. In the words of Pope Francis, how do we create a "culture of encounter," and overcome the "culture of indifference?"

Relationships, short or long-lived, in business, in church, in the chance meeting—all hold the promise of something invaluable. To be "in communion" with one another, through a sale, a conversation, an exchange of information or delegation of authority, is to take seriously the idea of Christ among us. Treating relationships in this way is not a utilitarian exercise, hoping for the consequence of better things to come. It is a gift of self and a way to live out a most important Christian duty: to be Christ for one another. For the EOC businesses in this study, daily encounters between buyers and sellers, between co-workers, between the business and the community, are as good a place as any in which to give and to receive Christ's love. It may be in this subtle appreciation and approach to relationships that other businesses have the most to learn from the EOC.

Another message evident in this look at EOC businesses is more implied than explicitly stated. It has to do with owners who have made a choice, at the cost of pursuing other opportunities, to do business their way. None of these business owners—creators of computer software, consultants, engineers, farmers, tour guides, teachers, trainers, cleaners, and makers of fine musical instruments—is exempt from the duties of management, the demands of competitive markets, the challenges of interpersonal relationships, the need to control costs and earn revenue. This is business. This is what they do. Yet they have chosen freely to participate in the Economy of Communion, which could be seen as simply another layer of non-revenue generating complication in an already burdensome endeavor. What, then, does EOC membership give them? I wonder if it isn't the chance to solve the problem of the divided life.

The divided life is one that confines expressions of faith in God to the Sabbath and to private expression, sealed and neatly separated so as not to contaminate the faith to which we have ceded the other six days: faith in the wisdom of markets, in the pursuit of self-interest and in happiness derived from material success. The man or woman who chooses to come to work whole on Monday, ready to work but also ready to examine work life, practices, policies, products and services in the light of truth and Christian values, does so at some peril. For such a person, especially one who has made no effort to hide this perspective, the foibles, mistakes and poor judgment which beset us all will quickly be cited as evidence of hypocrisy and insincerity when the failures are theirs. Worse, the very faith they sought to honor in the wholeness of their work may be slandered as the real culprit. It is in some ways easier to be one person at work and another person at home than to fight for authenticity and wholeness. But not to fight, to give in to the divided life has high costs of its own: in the short run, to feel daily conflicts of conscience and judgment; in the long run, alienation and loss of personal identity.

This, I think, is the great lesson and appeal of the EOC and the lesson of *Structures of Grace*, especially for small business owners and startup businesses. Business, if it is to be a humanizing influence in society, must be rooted in a cultural soil that draws upon the graces that can structure business toward authentic human development. Without such an embedded reality, business eventually defaults to a narrow form of instrumental rationality focused only on efficiency and profitability. EOC businesses stand as evidence that an integration of deep culture and business, of faith and work, are possible. The solution to the divided life is not putting all the pieces together in the right order in the life and work we have right now, but in seeking and claiming transcendent values which, by their scope and height and weight, are large enough to support the whole of our lives. Christ lives. And he lives among us!

Michael J. Naughton, Ph.D.
Professor, Ethics and Business Law, Opus College of Business
Interim Director of the Center for Catholic Studies
University of St. Thomas
Minnesota

W hat motivates a person to start a business? Typical entrepreneurs can be driven by a number of factors—the desire to produce new products or services, a search for wealth and economic independence, or a need for creative expression. In a classic capitalistic viewpoint, one could say that the key motivation is to '*maximize the return on investment of the shareholders.*' In recent years, however, a new breed of entrepreneur has emerged—the social entrepreneur—whose motivation for starting a business is to fulfill some unmet need in the world, or to transform the world itself in a positive way through the activities of the business. This book by John Gallagher and Jeanne Buckeye attempts to shine light on one of the first and largest global social business networks resulting from the Economy of Communion, or the EOC for short. However, as you will discover, the EOC cannot be categorized simply as another economic activity of social entrepreneurs. It is much more than this.

Since emerging in the early 1990s from the desire to respond to the poverty found within a worldwide ecclesial community called the Focolare Movement[1], the EOC has grown to include over 860 small to medium-sized businesses in over 50 countries involving citizens, workers, scholars and students (more than 350 theses and dissertations written) and people in need. My wife Julie and I are owners of two of these EOC businesses. We are not typical entrepreneurs and never saw ourselves as 'business people'. Nor did we ever imagine that running a company would provide a means of fulfilling any of our greatest dreams and aspirations for ourselves or the world. However, when we met the Focolare thirty-five years ago while in college, we were introduced to its spiritual lifestyle of communion

---

1. See pages 19-20 for a brief description of the Focolare.

based on putting the lines of the Christian Gospel into practice in our everyday lives. Through living its principles we
have come to realize that our personal lives, faith lives, and
even our work lives are not separate realities, but instead
constitute one ongoing opportunity to bring meaning and
transformation within us and around us.

We are often asked by people who become interested in
the Economy of Communion what we think it has to offer
other business entrepreneurs in the United States today.
This question immediately reminds us of a quote from
the Acts of the Apostles that Chiara Lubich, foundress of
the Focolare Movement and the EOC, gave to us for our
company's operating motto when we joined this unique
initiative almost 20 years ago:

"There is more joy in giving than receiving." Acts 20:35

Joy—this is the gift the EOC gives! It is the happiness,
well-being and deep satisfaction that comes from living a
meaningful life integrated with our most heartfelt beliefs
and resulting from the relationships that grow out of this
giving and receiving. As Chiara has said to us: *"...human
beings find their fulfillment in loving, in giving. This need
is in the deepest recesses of their being, whether they have
faith or not."* From the beginning, our simple yet direct
motto focused us on the relationships we would build within
the company, with the local community near the company,
and with the world community.

These relationships are the key because one of the distinguishing characteristics of our EOC business lifestyle is
the fact that behind each moment of each business day, an
EOC business owner tries to live with a continuous awareness of the other person in order to create and maintain
a workplace and business *of communion.* Let's be honest
—there are many, many business owners in the world and
many socially-responsible companies that do 'good works'
with 'good hearts'. But that alone, for us in the EOC, is not

enough. We desire an added dimension, an intangible but nevertheless real product: *communion*. Everything else within the business flows from this—the production, the financial management, the sales and marketing, the human resources. And therein also lays the challenge—to accomplish *communion* within the day-to-day 'messy' realities of running a business: the successes and failures, the unexpected events, the employee resignations and firings, the late-paying clients.

The communion we build and rebuild over time is not some nebulous, idyllic, textbook concept, but a true, lived, concrete and essential reality that grows deeper and deeper as we take the steps towards each other in the daily happenings of our businesses. How this actually happens within the EOC companies in North America is the primary focus of this book. We hope that John and Jeanne's efforts herein help others more fully understand and appreciate this added dimension of work-life that is open to everyone.

John Mundell,
President/CEO, Mundell & Associates
November 2014

Preface

When we first met Andre Roberge, the owner of Arc-en-Saisons (a commercial services firm you will come to know in the pages of this book), one of the things he said, upon learning we were college professors was; "You must write a book about the Economy of Communion!" Our immediate response to Andre was, "And you must be in it!"

Both of these things have happened. A book has been written and Andre is indeed in it. But when one undertakes to write yet another "business" book, and offer it to contemporary readers, one should be prepared to defend the undertaking. Business books abound; and so the question as to what this book has to offer is important. Allow us to make four observations about contemporary life that provide insight as to why we wrote this book, and why (we think) you should read it.

First, business is one of the dominant institutions of modern life. But we moderns (at least in the United States) are of two minds when it comes to the way we think about business. Businesses, and business executives, are not universally admired or enthusiastically embraced. Common concerns might be centered on questions of corporate greed and profiteering, as well as invasive advertising and relentless marketing. Recent news reports raise questions of patriotism by vilifying U.S. corporations for acquiring overseas companies in order to escape taxation. At the same time, a well respected company like Apple can release a new smartphone to widespread admiration and acclaim for its technological savvy and innovative prowess. There are some companies we love, and we celebrate their contributions to our lives. Others, some of whom we have admired in the past, now seem to earn nothing but our scorn.

Second, it is not then surprising that abstract questions about the role and responsibilities of business are contested. What should be our expectations of private enterprise companies? Perhaps they should serve their owners as profit seeking entities; perhaps they should focus on customers, looking to meet various needs and wants no matter how questionable or self-serving those may be. Perhaps they should be viewed as providers of jobs and a means of livelihood for the millions of employees who work for them. Certainly, over the past several decades, ideas about the social responsibility of business have gained traction, and pointed our attention toward environmental concerns and sustainability. And what of the rise, over that same time period, of social ventures, benefit corporations, and innovative forms of public-private partnerships? As a society, do these sometimes conflicting and mutually exclusive ideas about the responsibility of business cause confusion and dysfunction?

Third, we might be described as enamored of entrepreneurship particularly with high-tech startups and IPO's. Countless municipalities and states are actively looking to promote new ventures in our communities, to entice some of us to take the risk and launch companies of our own. A life lived in the entrepreneurial world can be both maddening and exhilarating. The work is complex, demanding, rewarding, unpredictable, sobering, fulfilling, larger than life, stretching, and risky. Indeed, it is life in a crucible; a life of formation, both burdensome and liberating. Starting and running a business shapes a person. It becomes part of who you are, and how you see yourself, and how others see you.

Fourth, and finally, for young people, such a world may indeed look complex and intimidating. And to that complexity, they bring questions informed by their dreams, and values, and by their fears. Many of them have watched us live divided lives where we must be a certain person in the business world, but a different one at home, or with friends. The question of personal values and faith in the workplace is huge, and hugely important; so much so, that the Supreme Court sees fit to weigh in, clarifying rights and responsibilities as they relate to personal and religious conviction. Young people wonder if the demands of this complex world will force them to adopt modes of behavior they might regret. Into all this, the Economy of Communion (EOC) speaks with a fresh—and refreshing—voice!

We wrote this book to give expression to that voice. As experienced professors in business, both of us at religiously affiliated institutions of higher education, we have regularly engaged our students, and our alumni who have gone on to become accomplished business professionals, with these types of complex and profound questions. Collectively, we have been teaching for over 50 years, and we bring nearly 30 more years of corporate experience to that teaching, so our engagement with these practicalities constitutes more than a single lifetime.

We recognized that the EOC was a fresh voice, and from our earliest acquaintance with its people we hoped to play a part in telling the story of the EOC to a wider audience. We wanted to bring that voice to a wider audience, to help that voice speak into these questions.

This book is a first step; a milestone marker along the path of a journey. Dozens of events, scores of people, hundreds of conversations, and thousands of hours both defined and made possible this journey. For us, the journey will continue. What we hope to do here is to, in some small way, express our gratitude to everyone who made all, or parts, of the journey with us, and to all who might read this book and continue the journey from here. The people who made all or part of this journey gave of their time, energy, insight, work, wisdom, and wit. Some folks were with us for the longest parts of that journey, others were only brief sojourners. But all of them—and each of them—earned our eternal gratitude. And so, we'd like to say thanks to each of them, somewhat in order of the magnitude of their participation.

We first have to say thanks to all of the Economy of Communion (EOC) business owners who participated in this study. This would include, of course, Andre Roberge, and his wife Celine; Anne Godbout of Spiritours and her husband, Fernando (now proud parents of a baby boy Samuel); Nick Sanna from Netuitive; Joan Duggan from Finish Line; Miriam Turri of LaParola; Roger Krokey from Terra Nuova; Sue Paroski, and her husband, Tom, of First Fruits Farm; John Welch of Sofia Violins (Consort International); Ed Brown from DealerFlow Corporation; Claude Blanc of CHB; Paulina Sennett of Ideal Safety Communications; Phil Solinsky of the Solinsky Financial Group; and finally John Mundell, and his wife Julie, of Mundell and Associates. Before this book began, John and his company, Mundell & Associates, were the subject of a business case study we published in 2011 in *The Case Research Journal*. John and Julie are the EOC business owners we have known the longest, and the ones who kindly introduced us to other EOC owners. We owe both of them a special acknowledgement.

Each of these business owners not only answered our questionnaires and telephone queries, but also met with us, formally and informally, at more than one annual EOC meeting. Many of them hosted us at their place of business, allowed us to talk with their employees, suppliers, and even some customers. Some welcomed us into their homes, and introduced us to their families and their children. So, unquestionably, this is their book. And our gratitude to each of them is immense.

A number of Focolare members have also been inordinately helpful to us on this journey. Some of them are closely involved with the EOC, some not. But all of them contributed greatly to our understanding. First among them would have to be Terry Gunn and Amy Uelmen. Sadly, Terry passed away in 2011, but not before he spent the better part of two days patiently explaining the Focolare spirituality of unity in ways that made it accessible. Amy, of course, started all this back in 2005. Our debt to these two is profound.

But there were countless others; some we met at annual EOC meetings, or at academic conferences, or as part of our field research. Among these are Elizabeth Garlow, now at Princeton University; Linda Specht at Trinity University in San Antonio; Gary Brandl; Judith Povilus and the students at Sophia University in Loppiano; Lorna Gold; Fr. Pete Iorio; Jim and Jane Milway; Alejandra Marinovic Gujon and Alvarao Vercelli, both in Santiago, Chile; Bettina Gonzalez, of Boomerang Viajes in Buenos Aires; Sr. Helen Alford; Luigino Bruni; Guiseppi Argiolas; Maria Balderelli; and Katerina Ferrone. There are more to be sure. It would be impossible to name them all, and there were some with whom we spoke and from whom we never got a name. But to all of them, we are grateful.

Both of us have close colleagues who did us the huge favor of listening to our ideas, reading our work, sitting through presentations, offering comments, insight, support, and encouragement. Among these are Mike Naughton, Ken Goodpaster, and Bob Kennedy, from the University of St. Thomas, Tricia Bruce at Maryville College, Michael Gallagher at Fairfield University, Jenny Fowler at the University of Tennessee, and Andrew Abela at Catholic University of America. In addition, there were numerous attendees at presentations during our research, including colleagues at Fordham University, Catholic University of America, Maryville College, and the University of St. Thomas. And we are grateful for the incredible institutional support we enjoyed from both Maryville College and the University of St. Thomas, particularly the John A. Ryan Institute.

We are grateful to New City Press for agreeing to publish this work, seeing it as a modest contribution to a greater understanding of EOC principles and practices. Jim Webber, in particular, has been, open, accessible, and wise, and in short, a joy to work with, and Tom Hartmann, patiently plowed through the manuscript, editing, and improving, and much credit for what you hold in your hands goes to both of them.

This book is equally co-authored and so we owe a significant debt to each other, and to our families and friends, for endless patience and good cheer through the long days of writing, traveling, analyzing, and rewriting. For John, a special debt of gratitude is owed to his wife Pat, a constant companion on the journey, and as always, the first among God's many gifts. At least for her, this was an opportunity to travel to Italy; to Rome, and to Loppiano, and become enchanted with *il dulce far niente!* For Jeanne, special thanks go to Mary, dearest daughter and number one friend; to sister, Kathy, who has a limitless supply of loving encouragement; and to then 8 year-old Andrew, who, after listening attentively to a description of the research, solemnly promised, "Aunt Jeanne, when your book gets published I am going to buy a copy!" Bless him. Bless them all.

Finally, we know that God makes all things possible. Making this journey was a blessing, and a grace, and to Him, the author of unity, we give our praise and thanks.

Introduction

I t's difficult to pinpoint where and when we first became aware of the Economy of Communion, but our active involvement with Economy of Communion (EOC) companies began in the summer of 2007. In June of that year, one of us traveled to Indianapolis to meet with the owner and founder of the company, Mundell & Associates. That meeting eventually led to our starting work on a case study of Mundell (published in late 2011). But it also led to everything else. We attended our first North American EOC annual meeting in 2008, and have been active participants in various EOC meetings and conferences since then.

The specific impetus for this book grew out of our experience with that first case study. At that time, we thought we might be able to produce one case study per year and eventually have enough material to produce a descriptive study much like the one you hold in your hands. We realized quickly that to do so might take us ten or twelve years, and that a better course might be to involve a small number of companies in a structured research project aimed at understanding the particular ways of doing business that are unique to an EOC business. The general outline for such a project was developed during the summer of 2008, and we started work in earnest that same fall after securing agreements to participate from some fourteen EOC companies in both the United States and Canada. Since the specifics of this research journey are chronicled in detail later, let us just say here that it has been a fascinating journey, indeed, in some respects, a life-changing journey.

One of the persistent struggles we faced during this project was to keep our work focused on *description*. From the very beginning, the idea of comparing EOC companies in some way to other companies, or of evaluating and judging whatever business practices we might encounter against some identifiable standard of best practice was a persistent temptation. But at the same time this seemed to be the wrong road to go down at this time. Partly this was because any *comparison* or *judgment* would have come loaded with significant assumptions, many of them unclear or necessarily unspoken.

First of all, comparison or judgment would require an assumption that there indeed exists an identifiable set of best business practices against which we could say that EOC practices are the same or "better" or "worse," Further, it assumes that we could group all these EOC companies into one group and then all other business in the world into another group. This seemed a bit artificial and possibly futile.

We also were grappling with coming to a solid understanding of our own about the EOC and were also encountering other people who experienced some difficulty in understanding the project. As one of our business owners remarked, the EOC is not easy to understand. We found, as did he, that the most common reaction of others unfamiliar with the EOC is to look for comparisons. We routinely encountered people who very quickly wanted to slot the EOC somewhere: for instance, into the corporate social responsibility movement; into social entrepreneurship; or into a sophisticated version of a non-profit organization. Moreover, the faith element made many people skeptical and provoked what seemed to us a rush to judgment.

As our own understanding of the EOC grew and deepened, we realized that the EOC was being shortchanged by such attempts at comparison and judgment. The EOC does not simply embody some other comparable set of standards or practices. It is not just another form of social responsibility or philanthropy. It is not just another version of visionary leadership, or servant leadership, or charismatic leadership.

It is not simply another adaptation of faith principles to business.

No, the richness and uniqueness of the EOC needed to be described in its own right and not as just similar to something else. Let's be clear. Such comparisons and judgments can be made, and eventually should be made, but not without first gaining a clear and uncluttered picture of what the EOC is like. And so, we worked hard to maintain our focus on description. This does not mean we provide no reflection or analysis, but we try to produce a clear and credible synthesis of what we learned about the ways these companies conduct their business and manage their companies.

We have, for the most part, opened each chapter with some reference to management and business literature, but mostly as a way of framing and drawing attention to particular business practices. This is not an exhaustive study. It does not document every last conceivable practice. It deals rather with selected business practices, and so in each case we provide some background and context for the relevance of any particular practice. Why marketing, for example; or, why hiring practices, or competitive practices, or leadership practices? Our exposition of the importance of these particular practices is therefore grounded in the literature.

The book unfolds in eight chapters. Chapter One lays out our rationale for the project, but also includes a short history of the Economy of Communion and a theoretical reflection that provides some suggestions of what we might find. For as much as we have already talked about maintaining a focus on description, we do very much have some findings to report. This chapter draws from the literature to speculate on what these might be. And, for the sake of clarity we have articulated what we might find as follows. We might find that EOC companies are no different from any other companies—that there is nothing here in any way new or noteworthy. We might find that there is much variety in business practices among our EOC companies, or that there

is such a great deal of uniformity among them that there is
an identifiable EOC way of doing business. Much of this
theoretical development appeared in a paper we presented
in May of 2010 in Loppiano, Italy. That paper appeared as
a chapter in the book, *The Charismatic Principle in Social
Life*, edited by Bruni and Sena, and published by Routledge
in the fall of 2102.

Chapter One also contains a short description of each
of the subject companies that includes some remarks about
the products and services they provide. There were a total
of fourteen companies included in this study. Those com-
panies are Mundell & Associates and Sofia Violins (Con-
sort), both in Indianapolis IN; Finish Line in Hyde Park,
NY; Terra Nuova in Rhinebeck, NY; First Fruits Farm in
Los Angeles, CA; Dealerflow in Kokomo, IN; Ideal Safety
Communication in Chicago, IL; Netutive in Reston, VA;
Spiritours in Montreal, Ontario, Arc-en-Saisons in Granby,
Ontario; La Parola in Denver, CO; The Solinsky Financial
Group in Tucson, AZ; Techquest, Inc. in Houston, TX; and
CHB Consulting in Freehold, NJ. One company, Techquest,
did not participate in the study at all due to the death of
the owner at the very start of the project. Of the remaining
thirteen companies, eight completed and returned every
survey we sent out, but all data provided by every company
was used in the development of this manuscript.

Chapter Two, then, documents marketing practices and
Chapter Three, competitive practices. Both of these chapters are primarily external in perspective; that is, how these
EOC companies engage with the world around them, with
their customers and competitors, and in some cases suppliers. Chapter Four turns inward and explores the nature and
design of work inside these EOC companies and examines
how these companies actually get their work done. Chapter
Five examines the practices surrounding employment, both
hiring and training, and also orientation of new employees
particularly toward EOC values. Chapter Six takes on the

question of company culture and leadership, while Chapter Seven considers the effect of crises, or defining moments, in the life of these businesses. And finally, Chapter Eight presents our reflections, conclusions, and preliminary answers to the question, "What, in essence, is the Economy of Communion?"

Generally, the Economy of Communion is known by its acronym, EOC. We have elected to use the acronym in most places throughout the manuscript although there are certain places where we elect to use the full name because it either retained the integrity of the data or it seemed to us to provide the appropriate emphasis. There is one other item of note we should mention, in regard to the use of footnotes. Where we have quoted or used material from published public sources we have provided full footnotes and a complete list of references. Beyond that, all of the material is gleaned either from our surveys or our conversations with these business owners, their employees, and sometimes their suppliers and customers. Where we have either quoted directly from one of these or substantively paraphrased something they have said, we have also provided footnotes that indicate whether the source was a survey or a focus group or a conversation during one of our field studies. Certainly large portions of the text are not directly footnoted but these are where we have synthesized and interpreted the material ourselves. We are confident that those portions are a faithful rendition of the information provided to us.

Chapter One

Understanding the Economy of Communion

The Economy of Communion project is unique, and therefore not easy to define. One of the business owners who participated in this study claims this is partly because no one wants to take the time to understand it. But that's not the whole story. It takes more than just time. It takes serious investigation into its complexity and multiple dimensions, and reflection on the characteristics that make it unique. The Economy of Communion (EOC) resists comparisons with other phenomena. One can't simply say that it's just another example of corporate social responsibility or another form of social entrepreneurship. One can't say it's like a non-profit or a cooperative. It is like all of those things in some ways but it is not like those things in enough other ways that any comparison simply doesn't hold.

There are a number of things that contribute to this uniqueness. One is that the EOC is grounded in faith and spirituality. The EOC attempts not just to live out the faith convictions of the business owners, but also to be a concrete expression of the "spirituality of unity" of the Focolare. Further, it is an attempt to live out the faith and social teachings of the Catholic Church and, in particular, the preferential option for the poor. Another contributing factor is that the EOC places profits in common. Unlike individual companies that may distribute a portion of their profits to worthy causes, the EOC distributes profits in order to create a "communion of goods" that can be shared with those in need. Individual business owners surrender a significant

13

measure of control over the distribution of their profits. The EOC also encourages business owners to view their companies as communities—entities defined by personal relationships—and to manage accordingly.

Simply put, the EOC is out to change the world. For these companies, changing the world means "humanizing" the economy by consistently privileging relationships over profit-maximizing, and by putting profits in common and using them to address acute social needs and concerns. It also means "humanizing" companies and organizations through business practices that respect the inherent dignity of each person, and that are aimed at breaking down barriers between people in business. Given this, EOC business owners have thought, and continue to think, very seriously about some very important questions. While many of the businesses are small, with very concentrated private ownership, the business owners have faced, and continue to face, the questions about the nature, role, and purpose of business, and the economic, social, and moral responsibilities of business. They have thought deeply about these issues and, of course, they act on these issues daily, and their insights, observations, and experiences, offer lessons far greater than the size of any single business. They bring a strong, clear, seasoned voice to any discussion about the proper role of business in the larger society.

These multiple dimensions and high ideals contribute to the challenge of defining or understanding the EOC. Adding to that challenge is that the fact that the EOC makes claims about itself. It claims to be a new style of economic action. It claims to be an antidote, or a prescription for an antidote, to *homo oeconomicus*. It claims to offer a different understanding of economic life that might be particularly relevant at a time when many parts of the world are recovering from one of the more severe economic downturns in our history that was perhaps precipitated by an incomplete or faulty understanding of economic activity.[1]

Taken together, all of these characteristics contribute to the difficulty of defining the EOC. Yet, two of the most common questions we are asked whenever we encounter people unfamiliar with this project are, "What is the EOC?" and "Are EOC companies any different?" The first of these questions arises from the characteristics we've already pointed out. The second bears some further consideration. When people ask if EOC companies are any different, we often find that question to be asked in two fundamentally different ways. One is hopeful, the other cynical.

When asked out of hope, the question really reflects a desire to believe there are examples of good corporate behavior—and examples of companies that are really valued and revered by their customers and employees. Many of us (as customers and as employees) have had positively exhilarating and affirming experiences with companies that suggest there are good corporate citizens. And there are some possible companies of legend here: Apple, Southwest Airlines, or Patagonia, to name a few. *Fortune* magazine routinely identifies great companies to work for, and we all have products that we think are incredibly useful and a delight to use or consume. When the EOC is questioned in this hopeful manner perhaps it reflects a desire to believe that EOC companies must be of the same kind.

But, more often than not, the question is posed out of cynicism, with an expectation that business is business, and there is very little room for idealistic companies amid the fierce demands of competition. Here too we have the examples of WorldCom, or Enron, or Tyco. The profit motive taints everything and prompts the conviction that it is only naiveté that permits any thought that companies can be good

---

1. Gold, Lorna. 2010. *New Financial Horizons: The Emergence of an Economy of Communion.* Hyde Park: New City Press. p 36.

citizens. It's reflective of despair that companies can ever be anything other than greedy, deceitful, and manipulative and of the popular perception of business that companies will let us down. They will treat us without dignity and respect, pull the wool over our eyes, get as much from us as possible, tell us as little as possible, and make as much money as possible for themselves.

Both of these competing views, the hopeful and the cynical, can be found in the academic literature. For, in the particular case of the EOC, these competing questions are ways of asking if EOC companies are shaped by the values, beliefs, and convictions of the owners, and by the Focolare spirituality of unity, that is, shaped by "internal" forces. Or are they shaped by the fierce competition of the marketplace, that is, by external forces? The idea that organizations are, and can be, reflective of values or shaped by internal factors owes much to the work of Philip Selznick. In his classic book, *Leadership and Administration*, Selznick argues that organizations are shaped by the characteristics, values, beliefs, and commitments of the people who make up the organization.[2] Moreover, he argues that the organization is shaped partly by its own history; past actions and decisions can and do determine present and future actions. His argument rests on his distinction between two fundamentally different types of organizational behaviors or practices.

The first of these are behaviors governed by the "logic of efficiency," that is, "rational, means-oriented, and efficiency grounded," He labels this behavior as "administrative." The second of these is behavior governed by shared beliefs and values and is "value-laden, adaptive, and responsive." He labels these behaviors as the process of "institutionalization."[3]

2.   Selznick, Philip. 1957. *Leadership in Administration*. New York: Harper & Row, and also Scott, W. Richard. 1981. *Organizations: Rational, Natural, and Open Systems*, Prentice Hall. Englewood Cliffs, New Jersey, 3e. p 65.
3.   Perrow, Charles. 1986. *Complex Organizations: A Critical Essay*. New York: Mc-Graw-Hill. 3e. p 167. But here Perrow also references Selznick, "Foundations of a Theory of Organizations," *American Sociological Review*, 13, 1948. Perrow contrasts

And, he views organizational leadership as largely concerned with choosing between these two processes; administration and institutionalization. In the administrative process organizational leadership is called upon to "design" behavior, to rationally anticipate what is needed and to design appropriate responses and solutions and plans. There is intentionality about organizational practices. In the institutionalization process there is a recognition that not all things can be anticipated and leaders are called upon to respond to unforeseen challenges and circumstances and unplanned events and to respond or adapt. In this process, adaptation over time becomes habitual. As an organization and its people respond in these habitual ways the behavior becomes shared. In the instance of response, the leader relies on values and deeply held beliefs and convictions. In this way the organization becomes a reflection of those values and beliefs. In this way, the organization becomes what it does and becomes a function of its own history.[4]

Selznick is arguing that as organizations, leaders, and members encounter and interact with the external environment, they can respond and adapt by relying on and refining their values as they go. At some point, that value-laden adaptation becomes institutionalized and becomes the identity of the organization.[5]

Over against this idea is the notion that external forces are so strong and so demanding that they will eventually force organizations to respond and adapt in very similar, if not identical, ways, such that values and beliefs are trumped by the need to satisfy external demands. For Max Weber, the external demand was efficiency. He believed that in a capitalist market economy, the competitive process that all organizations would face would place a priority on efficiency

---

the "economic" aspect of an organization with its "institutional" aspect—which we take to mean "social." Put Review in italics.

4. Perrow, p 158.
5. Selznick, p 16.

and force all organizations into bureaucratic structures and practices and that would promote and achieve efficiency.[6] This is Weber's "iron cage." The central idea is that the demand of the external environment for economic organizations was competition and competition would eventually produce "homogeneity" in organizational practices. Every organization would act the same way. Later scholars, particularly Meyers and Rowan, began to use the term "isomorphism" to describe this phenomenon. Meyers and Rowan also argued that the drive for legitimacy might be stronger than the drive for efficiency.[7] In other words, it was not just competitive markets that were shaping firms, but emulation. When organizations grew in stature, or respect, or that grew to be trusted, this conferred some legitimacy on their practices. Other organizations would emulate those practices in order to achieve the same legitimacy, the same trust and respect.

DiMaggio and Powell enlarged this line of thinking by suggesting that while "homogenization" (or isomorphism) was inevitable,[8] it could be driven by coercive forces such as governments and state agencies or by mimetic forces such as suggested by Meyer and Rowan or by normative forces such as education and professional organizations that would tend to promote standardized acceptable norms of behavior. Di Maggio and Powell also introduced the idea of "decoupling"; that is, that organizations might appear to act one way—appear to be acting in ways that might confer legitimacy (normative or mimetic forces)—but in reality

---

6. Weber, Max. 1968. *Economy and Society: An Outline of Interpretive Sociology.* New York: Bedminster Press.
7. Meyer, J.W., and Rowan, B. 1977. Institutionalized Organizations: Formal structure as myth and ceremony. *American Journal of Sociology,* 83: 357.
8. DiMaggio, P.J. and Powell, W.W. 1983. "The Iron Cage Revisited: Institutional Isomorphism and Collective Rationality in Organizational Fields." *American Sociological Review,* Vol. 48, No. 2.

might be pursuing efficiency. So companies could appear to be legitimate, but underneath be ruthless.

We argue, and indeed it is the premise of this book, that finding answers to these important questions about the EOC must begin with examining the *business practices* of these companies. It is here, in the day-to-day challenge of pursuing success and sustainability that we can begin to define and understand the EOC, and begin to formulate conclusions about whether EOC companies are any different. As Luigino Bruni says about the EOC in the introduction to the volume, *The Economy of Communion: Toward a Multi-Dimensional Economic Culture*:

> It has to be said, however, that no matter how renewed and enriched the concepts of economic science are, they will never be able to comprehend a reality like the Economy of Communion in its entirety. A living reality can only be understood through continuous recourse to real life experience and, therefore, through visiting those businesses that are participating and by entering, at least a little, into the daily routine of these men and women... [9]

This book is intended to be just such a recourse to the real life experiences of EOC business owners in North America, and just such a way of entering "at least a little" into the daily routine of these men and women. What follows is a brief history of the EOC and the development of its business ideas, followed by a full descriptive introduction to each of the unique companies that agreed to participate in this study.

The History of the Economy of Communion

The Economy of Communion grew out of the social and spiritual vision of Focolare, a lay, Catholic, ecclesial movement active in more than 140 countries. The Focolare

---

9. Bruni, Luigino. 2002. *The Economy of Communion: Toward a Multi-Dimensional Economic Culture*. Hyde Park: New City Press, p 12.

itself began in 1943 in Trent, Italy. Amid the bombed ruins of their city and homes, Chiara Lubich and a small group of friends prayed together, read the Bible and shared what food and material goods among themselves and offering what they could to others. Eventually they came to believe that "God is the only value worth living for,"[10] and that they were called to live out the prayer that Jesus prayed the night before he died: "Father, may they all be one."[11] They expressed this new "spirituality of unity" by living in community, holding possessions in common and sharing generously with anyone in need. Almost immediately, the Focolare began to spread and grow, even during the war; afterwards it quickly spread beyond Italy. Today Focolare includes men, women and children in all parts of the world, of all faiths and beliefs. Some live together in community. Their prayer and work is directed toward promoting understanding, mutual respect, and love among peoples, and to establishing a "culture of giving" that stands in contrast to what they term the contemporary "culture of having."

On a visit to Sao Paulo, Brazil, in 1991, Lubich observed the significant unmet material needs of Focolare members living in and among the favelas there. In concert with others in the movement, she determined to address the local movement assembly, and after a moving speech on the need for action, issued a call for an "economy of communion."[12] Almost immediately Focolare launched EOC

---

10. Gallagher, Jim. 1997. *Chiara Lubich: A Woman's Work: The Story of the Focolare Movement and its Founder.* New City Press. Hyde Park, NY. On page 31, Gallagher reports, "One thing on which they had all agreed was that in this life everything would pass. Only God endured, only God was eternal. Everything else was vanity."
11. Jn:17:21.
12. It's not clear when the phrase "economy of communion" was first used. To our knowledge, the exact text of Chiara Lubich's call in Brazil in 1991 is preserved only on videotape, but it is also well documented in subsequent texts. One is particular is Lubich, Chiara. 1999. "The Experience of the Economy of Communion: A Proposal for Economic Action from the Spirituality of Unity," presented at the Strasbourg Conference of Political Movements for Unity. May 1999, and included in Bruni, Luigino. 2002. *The Economy of Communion: Toward a Multi-Dimensional Economic Culture.* Hyde Park: New City Press, p 15.

and willing business people came forward to participate. Initially the call was to accomplish what charitable giving alone could not: to generate enough money to provide for the poor, at a minimum the poor who participated in the Focolare. Through economic activity EOC would increase the "communion of goods" available to be shared through the creation of competently managed businesses that could provide jobs and generate profits. A portion of those profits would be held in common and distributed to those in need.

Formally known as the "Economy of Communion in Freedom," the project invited companies to compete like any other business, locally and globally, and to participate freely in the ideals of the movement. Going beyond a purely transactional view of economic activity, the EOC understood communion or unity to be the true objective of business activity; markets were valuable not for buying and selling alone, but more importantly as places for interpersonal encounter and relationship.[13] To those ends, the EOC "ideal" placed "persons" at the center of the enterprise. The ideal also held the need for a three-part distribution of profits among participating business owners. One part of profits must be reserved for reinvestment in the business to support a capacity for efficiency, competitiveness and sustainability. A second part would go to the EOC to be used in common for activities that promoted a "culture of giving" and advanced the work of the EOC itself. The final share of profits, to be held by the EOC in common, would be reserved for job creation and meeting material needs of those who share a belief in the spirit of the project.[14]

By 2010, the EOC project included over 750 businesses worldwide. Most are small, entrepreneurial, businesses that are integral members of their local communities. Widely dispersed though they are, owners communicate regularly

13. Lubich, 1999, in Bruni, L. ed. 2002, p 17.
14. This is from their current website (http://www.edc-online.org/).

and freely share information with each other. EOC has preserved the emphasis on freely chosen participation, and
has remained relatively non-prescriptive with respect to the
business owners. A set of general principles articulates their
understanding of good business management[15] and emphasizes that business should be a place of "unity, manifesting a
culture of communion" among, employees, customers, suppliers, local community, investors and trustees. The EOC
includes numerous companies that are not only successful
competitors committed to good management practices, but
that stand also as manifestations of faith intentionally integrated and "lived" in the business world.

The Development of EOC Business Ideals

As the EOC grew from these early days in Sao Paulo
to the nearly 800 businesses we find today, the ongoing
experiences of business owners and managers altered
perceptions about business and opened them to insight and
understanding. The spirituality essentially called them to
reexamine and rethink basic business practices. As Lorna
Gold explains,

> The EOC was not simply about making profits to share with
> the poor, but applying the Focolare spirituality in the busi-
> ness, which meant "humanizing" economic structures, start-
> ing with the business as the basic unit of economic activity.[16]

This wasn't just about redistributing profits but about
a way of doing business, a way of living. Full participation of the EOC was a call to transform a business from an
economic entity to a social entity and to reconsider business not just as an activity with instrumental value but with

---

15. These are posted on the website, but they are also in a paper from Lorna Gold. Conference of the WCC/WLF/WARC/CEC/RvK. Economy in the service of life, Amersfoort, June 18, 2002.
16. Gold, Lorna. 2010. *New Financial Horizons: The Emergence of an Economy of Communion.* Hyde Park: New City Press, p 129.

intrinsic value.[17] So, the history of the EOC is also a history of thinking about business as a community of persons and as an enterprise motivated primarily by spirituality and not economics. The economic function is the context in which community is to be realized. It is precisely this call that leads us to suggest that EOC companies are *"structures of grace."*

This understanding of business was the result of a process that involved (and continues to involve) the sharing of experience, a great deal of both individual and collective reflection, a desire to live this ideal, and to realize the increase in the communion of goods. This process is manifest in the ongoing effort of the EOC business owners to articulate the principles and guidelines they have learned and that express their deepest aspirations. These principles rest on fundamental values of relationships, resource sharing, participative work environments, open communication, and the inherent dignity of each person.

EOC business owners conceive of business as a community. Every business prescribes a particular set of particular relationships and the business has a primary responsibility to nurture this set of relationships and to be ever mindful of this community. The business, by virtue of being a business, creates a constellation or persons — employees, customers, shareholders, competitors, suppliers and others — and this entire constellation of persons is a unique and dynamic community. Managing such an undertaking favors transparency, sensitivity, creativity, and imagination.

The attitude that EOC business owners bring to their day-to-day business life is very particularized. They subscribe to this lofty and abstract ideal but they put it into practice one person, one circumstance at a time. The abstract ideal doesn't find its way into a set of policies or guidelines or precedents, but rather in meeting the current needs of the

---

17. Gold, 2010, pp 128–132.

persons in the community as they encounter them, and where they encounter them, in the course of business. The first question business owners ask themselves in a business situation with another person is what need does this person have to give me, and what do I have to give to meet this need. And vice versa.

Given this, these business owners live in a world of tension—such as the tension that might arise between the interests of the business and the needs of members of the community. But they are not stressed nor are they paralyzed into non-action. Since the business creates a community, the interests of the business become something akin to a common good for the community. They seek congruence and make business decisions accordingly, a practice they describe as "seeing things together."

One aspect of the EOC that requires further elaboration is the attitude, practice, and mechanism that surround the redistribution of profits. Both the EOC and the larger Focolare movement have governance structures "headquartered" in Rome, Italy. For the EOC, the governance structure includes an International Commission that meets periodically in Rome and that is made up of members from all of the Focolare and EOC regions throughout the world. Thus, when the EOC talks about sharing profits with those in need, what they technically mean is that individual business owners provide funds from the profits of their business to the International Commission in Rome. This International Commission then distributes those funds based on the local and regional commission assessments of needs in the region—particularly among the Focolare in that region. So, it is not unusual to hear EOC business owners describe profit sharing as "sending money to Rome."

The EOC International Commission also engages in activities that are understood to be "spreading the culture of giving." These include maintaining the website, publishing books and periodicals, speaking engagements, conferences and other organized events, and the founding of Sophia University outside of Florence, Italy. Regional commissions also engage in many similar activities. Thus, there exists a somewhat formal accomplishment of two of the three parts to the EOC profit distribution commitment through the existing governance structure.

Subject Companies

We are fortunate in some ways that the companies who agreed to participate in this study are very diverse. Each of them provide very different products and services, and serve very different markets. They differ considerably in age, and in geographic location. What unites them is the EOC and its ideals, but each has a particular story to tell. In the pages that follow we provide a brief snapshot of each company. We have also provided the accompanying table (Table 1) to serve as a handy reference guide so that readers can refer back here time and again as they encounter the companies throughout the book. But let us introduce them.

Netuitive, Inc. — Though managed by EOC principles, Netuitive is unique among the companies in this study because of its ownership structure. As a privately held C corporation, 78 percent of Netuitive stock is owned by outside investors. Company revenues were $10 million in the most recent fiscal year. Netuitive's CEO is a Focolare member who emphasizes what he calls "the prophetic component" of the EOC philosophy, by which he means, "the values at the core (of EOC) that are more important than the technical issues."

TABLE 1. Participating Companies

Company Name	Products/ services	Location	Founded
Netuitive, Inc.	Software	Reston, VA	2002
Consort International (dba Sofia Violins)	Violins, violas, cellos	Indianapolis, IN	1989
Mundell & Associates, Inc.	Earth science and environmental consulting services	Indianapolis, IN	
Spiritours	Personal and Spiritual development trips and journeys	Montreal QC Canada	2003
eos Finish Line Inc.	Educational services, tutoring, workshops, evaluations	Hyde Park, NY	1992
Ideal Safety Communications, Inc.	Bilingual safety consulting services	Willowbrook, IL	2004
Dealerflow Corporation	Employee relationship management software	Kokomo, IN	2004
Arc-en-Saisons	Commercial cleaning and maintenance services	Granby QC Canada	2001
Terra Nuova Restorations	Ceramic restoration	Rhinebeck, NY	1993
First Fruits Farm	Livestock and agricultural products	Santa Paula CA	1994
La Parola	Italian language classes	Denver CO	1984
CHB Associates, LLC	Business development and executive coaching	Freehold NJ	2003

From headquarters in a Reston, Virginia, office complex, Netuitive communicates with sales teams located in New York, Chicago, Atlanta and London—cities chosen for their proximity to activity centers of large businesses and government agencies. Netuitive's customers and prospects are organizations that rely on internal electronic systems to deliver services (e.g., buying plane tickets via an internet travel business, using a credit card to pay on line, paying the credit card bill, etc.). Their software replaces methods that rely on probability rules to diagnose IT problems, using instead algorithms that actually learn the behavior of the applications they monitor allowing problems to be forecasted—and corrected—before systems fail. Its self-learning performance management software is designed to "replace(s) human guesswork with automated mathematics and analysis to understand normal system behavior across IT silos, isolate root causes and forecast problems for mission-critical applications."

Netuitive describes its product idea as an IT paradigm shift, and from this fact alone come some of the major challenges for company sales: overcoming resistance, educating the customer, capital budget timing, integration, and testing. The 50 full-time people employed at Netuitive, many of them engineers, share strong technical knowledge and skills. But corporate culture and values that support innovation, customer interaction, risk taking and work ethic have an equally important impact on their performance.

Consort International (dba Sofia Violins)—The oldest of the businesses participating in the study, Sofia Violins was founded two years before Chiara Lubich's call to start EOC businesses. The founder had been in the import business since the early 1980s, and was familiar with the challenges of trade practices in the Soviet countries. In 1988 he started a subsidiary to bring Bulgarian violins to the U.S. market, and soon began importing unfinished instruments from Bulgaria to be finished and sold from the company

headquarters in Indianapolis, Indiana. Today Sofia Violins
is a "maker of professional quality violins, violas and cellos" which it distributes worldwide through a network of
twenty-eight dealers in fine violins. The owner likes to
describe the company as a "(pre) Economy of Communion
company, managed according to EOC principles." Their instruments are made of premium naturally aged woods that
are purchased through associates in the Southern Balkans
and Western Europe. Products are individually and tradi-
tionally made.

The company is structured as a limited partnership between a US subchapter S corporation and a Bulgarian corporation, with the US company owning 79 percent and the
Bulgarian company owning 21 percent of the business. The
owner reports recent efforts to engineer a "quasi ESOP"
arrangement with the Bulgarian company to convert it to an
employee owned business. Three full time employees and a
part-time contractor are employed at the Indianapolis location and six full-time people work in the Bulgarian location.
They report revenue of approximately $450,000 in the most
recent fiscal year.

Mundell & Associates, Inc. — An "earth science and
environmental consulting services" company, Mundell &
Associates is another Indianapolis company. Founded in
1995, the company's owner is generally acknowledged as an
informal leader and coach/mentor among North American
EOC businesses. As a Focolare member since the 1970s, he
has a long commitment to the Focolare spirituality underlying the EOC idea. His lifelong entrepreneurial aspirations
were realized when he left a promising career with a large
environmental consulting business to start Mundell &
Associates, which he identified as an EOC business from
the start.

Mundell & Associates' owner had experience in estimating startup costs, having gone through the process
regularly in a previous job where he oversaw the startup

of 30 environmental consulting offices in various parts of the country. "We could start all of them for under $50K initially," he says, so that figure became the general funding estimate he used for Mundell & Associate's startup. Part of the startup would come from $30 thousand generated from the sale of stock in his former employer's company which he had earmarked for the new business. Startup costs were easy to estimate. The big unknown was revenue from consulting. To keep expenses down, he spent the first four months working out of an office in his home. Combined with frugal management and an early, continuous revenue flow, that initial investment met the business' early financing needs: 25 percent went to rent; 15 percent to equipment purchase and rental; 20 percent to supplies, insurance and professional fees; and another 20 percent to miscellaneous expenses. Mundell & Associates shared its first office space with another EOC company. When Mundell & Associates had too few staff to complete some projects in the early days, they subcontracted engineering and other services, a practice the company continues to use today.

Mundell & Associate's engineers and scientists conduct environmental site investigations and assessments, including water resource studies, geologic and hydrogeologic studies, chemical contamination assessments and human-health risk assessments. The business does soil and groundwater remediation and brownfield redevelopment, developing plans for drinking water protection, environmental management and regulatory compliance. In addition, Mundell & Associate's professionals offer litigation and expert witness services to industry, governments, engineering firms and lawyers. Structured as a subchapter S corporation, the company reported annual revenue of approximately $3.2 million for the latest fiscal year.

Spiritours—A Canadian company, Spiritours describes itself as "a unique tour operator specializing in personal and spiritual development trips and sacred journeys for small groups in the interest of equitable tourism." Their mission includes designing experiences with the idea of personal and spiritual growth in mind, offering travelers opportunities for personal reflection as they tour beautiful, sometimes exotic places around the world. Founded in 2003 as an EOC company, Spiritours is a Montreal business, privately owned.

Spiritours' founder and owner got the inspiration to start a tour company after having had a deeply spiritual experience on a journey of her own. For advice on how to get a business started she turned not to accountants, financial advisers, bankers or potential investors, but to family, friends and other entrepreneurs. Many of them remain close to the owner or are involved in Spiritours today. A sister, for example, supplied a model that became the basis for Spiritours' business plan; that sister continues to function as the owner's "coach." Her father has been there from the start "to listen and to counsel" his daughter, and he still leads at least one tour each year for the company. Before starting the business, Spiritours' owner worked for 11 years in another agency. Her former employer liked the concept of doing spiritual tours and had been encouraging from the start. He kept her employed part-time in his business as she was launching her own to ensure that she had income enough to live on. By establishing an affiliate relationship with Spiritours that lasted four years, he helped save the startup company the expense of insurance and agency permits when they could least afford them. The year she started Spiritours, the owner attended an EOC congress and sought out other EOC owners for advice. The owner of Finish Line Inc was especially helpful then and continues to be a special inspiration to her.

Spiritours' owner used personal savings to cover ninety-five percent of the startup financing; the other five percent came from revolving bank credit. The business ran very lean in the beginning, working via computer, phone and fax machine out of the owner's small condominium. When it finally became obvious that the condo space was too small to accommodate her and the staff she had hired, she sold the condo and used some of the proceeds to secure new space. Some proceeds also helped pay rent and salaries, set up an accounting system, buy insurance and establish a trust account. "When I started on my own," Spiritours owner reported, "our financing needs exceeded what I had imagined, but Providence always provided what was necessary."(18) Providence in this case and throughout is understood to be God's wonderful works on our behalf.

Most of Spiritours' clients live in Quebec, but tour groups often include people from other parts of Canada and the United States. The company has three full-time and two part-time employees, plus about 15 tour operators working on a contract basis for individual trips. The reported annual revenue for the most recent fiscal year was $2 million (Canadian).

eos Finish Line Inc. —Home to Finish Line is a tidy white frame house with brown trim, set on a wooded lot beside a windy country road in Luminosa, a Focolare community near Hyde Park, New York. The large driveway and parking area seem designed to welcome visitors, but little else indicates that these are the offices of an educational services company. Through a door near the parking area the visitor enters a small waiting room brightened with colorful furniture, artwork and inspirational posters. Just beyond is the office, headquarters for Finish Line Inc. From this quiet, rural location, Finish Line' provides one-on-one tutoring and related services, including evaluations for students, teachers and parents. One full time and one-part time employee oversee the work of up to 15 consultants hired on a temporary basis to tutor as needed during the school year. Though some work is SAT prep, the staff's primary focus is on high school and upper level middle school students who are simply trying to get passing grades. Students may be falling short for various reasons: learning differences, perhaps, a mismatch with teachers, poor skills or too little effort. In addition to the Luminosa location, Finish Line Inc. also offers its services from a second space in a nearby town.

Started in 1992, eos Finish Line Inc. was the first EOC company in North America. The founder, who was already active in Focolare, had been roused by Chiara Lubich's call to create EOC businesses. With successful entrepreneurial track records of her own, and professional experience in education, she believed she had a "fairly decent understanding of what it would probably take" to start a tutoring business. Relying heavily on prior experience, she also took the time to study information provided by the Small Business Administration, sought advertising advice from a friend in the business, and met with an accountant to be sure the business was properly set up. Financing of about $50 thousand came entirely from the owner's personal savings. She attached no terms or conditions to the money, regarding it as "a gift or no interest loan, depending on whether the business survived or not." Of this initial outlay, 20 percent paid for marketing and the rest went to salaries and benefits, and the money lasted "almost exactly until we started to sustain ourselves." Privately owned and incorporated, almost 20 years after its founding Finish Line remained a small business, reporting annual revenues of approximately one hundredand forty-five thousand.

Ideal Safety Communications, Inc. — As an OSHA "authorized outreach trainer" this EOC company operates in the arena of safety training for small and medium-sized businesses with bilingual (Spanish and English) workforces. A consulting business started in 2004 as a subchapter S corporation, Ideal has no outside owners or investors, and just one office location in Willowbrook, Illinois. The founder and owner is an experienced HR professional. The company has one part-time employee and occasionally contracts with others to do customized bilingual training. Technical translations and safety audits are also part of their services.

Dealerflow Corporation — As this research began in 2008, Dealerflow was an EOC company with a product but no revenue. Founded in 2004 to develop and market a human resource software tool, the business was the entrepreneurial brainchild of an HR/IT professional in Kokomo, Indiana. Dealerflow was launched as a sub-chapter S corporation with outside investors who owned 39 percent of the company. Their first product (employee relationship management software for automobile dealers), came to market in November 2008. But the company's struggle to correct performance issues in their first product, discovered in early implementation trials, slowed its efforts to finish designing an integrated software system of which this first product was only a part. As the study progressed, Dealerflow's prospects for survival dimmed. By the summer of 2010, with revenues inadequate to support ongoing development, DF had been forced to release its five full time employees, including the founder, and four part-time contractors. Among other options, investors were looking for a possible buyer for the business or its software.

Arc-en-Saisons — Arc-en-Saisons was the first EOC company in Canada. Founded in 2001, it operates in Granby, Quebec, providing painting, cleaning, landscaping, and mowing services primarily to commercial customers. At the start the owner envisioned developing a group of small service businesses managed under the Arc-en-Saisons banner. Looking for wise counsel on how to proceed, he discussed his ideas with an accountant, a lawyer, a banker and another entrepreneur, but all the conversations were disappointing. He explained that he wanted a way to organize his new business with a structure that somehow incorporated the EOC philosophy, but the concept seemed only to puzzle and distract the professionals. At a local business mentoring program staffed by retired executives, the consultants also had trouble grasping the business idea and the EOC connection. Finally he talked with a government agency dedicated to small business concerns, but the people there seemed uninterested or unable to understand too. His wife alone seemed to understand the business idea and the EOC connection, and in the end her support and encouragement was all he needed. Determined to go forward, he chose to organize Arc-en-Saisons in a standard corporate form, omitting mention of an EOC connection, and financing startup from personal savings. The company, he says, has never struggled financially and has provided him a good living. But the startup experience taught him that "people secure themselves in the structures that exist." Presented with something new, like the EOC, even professionals resist the effort to understand or accommodate the new thing.

Terra Nuova Restorations—Connected through the internet and personal networks to customers around the United States, Terra Nuova operates from a restored 80-year old stone house near Hyde Park, New York. This is a one-person operation, offering customers museum quality restoration of ceramic pieces. Trained and experienced in the art of ceramic restoration, the owner left a corporate job in 1993 to start Terra Nuova., turning what had been a hobby into a business. Before venturing out, however, he sought advice from several EOC business owners. One bit of counsel in particular struck home: "Start a company only if it can provide more income than what you can make as an employee." His own aspiration had been even more modest: to at least replace the salary he was making as a corporate manager. Believing that the new business could, indeed, provide that income was the deciding factor. The owner financed the startup with personal savings, correctly estimating that he would need less than $500 for incidental expenses to get things underway. He had no formal business plan, and sought advice only from an accountant to sort out tax questions related to distinguishing between business and personal expenses in a sole proprietorship. Within two years Terra Nuova satisfied the owner's desire to support himself and his family by doing the work he loves. The business is still small and the owner plans to keep it that way. He continues to work out of his home. Sometimes, he says, the company's size and modest plans for growth make him wonder if it is really even a business. Then he remembers the challenge of pleasing customers and the need to keep promoting his work, and decides that it sounds like a real business after all.

First Fruits Farm—In 1994, a high school math teacher living near Santa Paula, California became interested in starting a goat farm. She consulted with several business owners to get their thoughts about what it takes to run a livestock business. She liked what she heard and used their advice to establish First Fruits. Personal savings supplied the startup financing, about half of which went to purchase equipment, and the rest to buy livestock and supplies. Initial estimates for the cost of the animals were accurate, but she underestimated the cost of running a dairy—especially the vaccines, vets and special dietary needs of livestock. Despite that early surprise the business survived. Today First Fruits remains a small organic operation, providing goats and sheep, free range poultry and eggs. First Fruits' founder remains the sole owner and continues to do much of the work herself. On weekends she employs students from a nearby college to help with chores and get some experience in organic farming in the process.

La Parola—A native Italian living in Colorado, the owner of La Parola followed a friend's suggestion and put her language skills to work in starting a language studies business in 1984. It was, she says, an outgrowth of her desire to "help people live joyously the adventure of learning a new language." She uses her own home as a staging area to offer private Italian lessons for individuals and groups in the Denver, Colorado, area. One-on-one conversations carried on in the context of cooking classes, mountain hikes and other activities defined her unique approach. Startup involved a quick and virtually effortless decision, made with no business plan, no outside consultation and requiring no initial investment. A Focolare participant for many years when she heard about Chiara Lubich's call to establish EOC businesses, she simply chose to add La Parola to the EOC rolls. For her, it was not so much a new business as a new way of thinking about the business she was already running.

CHB Associates, LLC—In 2003 the founder of CHB left a corporate career to start an EOC business, turning years of experience in supervision, leadership, and coaching into an executive consulting firm that offers strategic consulting services to small and medium sized businesses. At startup, the founder of CHB relied on advice from company owners outside the EOC and worked with an accountant who recommended organizing as a limited liability corporation. Relying substantially on his own research and reading, CHB's owner planned a business that could "grow organically." He saw no need, therefore, for a plan projecting specific resource needs. Reassured by having secured a "substantial anchor client" at the start, CHB's founder confidently estimated the need for $35 thousand in startup funding. This he generated from multiple sources: personal savings a 10-year bank loan and revolving credit. The money would meet initial needs for equipment and supplies, marketing, training, and salaries and benefits. A native of France and a seasoned executive familiar with international business, the owner of CHB offers one-on-one coaching, group coaching and corporate teambuilding exercises. He contracts with individuals as well as businesses for his services. Because the executive coaching business requires significant networking and business outreach to generate clients, the company's New Jersey location, mid-way between Philadelphia and New York offers ideal proximity to a large pool of prospective corporate clients. This advantage plus the owner's connections from his days in a corporate setting, offer ample opportunities for generating business.

Looking Ahead

These are the EOC businesses that made this book possible and you will learn more about them, little by little in the chapters that follow. We maintain, as we've said before, that answers to the questions, "What is the EOC?" and "Are they different?" must begin with a snapshot of their business practices. Beyond the question of whether they are "different" we also don't know how similar or dissimilar they are to each other. Perhaps there is enough common ground among EOC companies, and enough distinction from "ordinary" companies to suggest an EOC way of doing business that is unique and different; or, perhaps not. Regardless, we also believe it important to produce a record, an historical, journalistic snapshot, of EOC companies at this particular point in time.

And, this is why you hold this volume in your hands. We set for ourselves the task of describing what goes on inside at least some EOC companies in North America on a daily basis. What are the business practices of the EOC? How do they make pricing, advertising, and marketing decisions? How do they make hiring and firing decisions? How do they develop employee and employment policies and practices? These are among the questions we have been asking EOC company owners in North America. Our analysis and reflection process convinced us that presenting our findings would be best done not by following the sequence of survey topics or any chronological approach, but by presenting data and analysis in chapters that both consolidate and integrate related topics. To that end, we begin with marketing because marketing is the generator of revenues, and for entrepreneurial businesses, with limited or specialized goods and services, an overriding question is whether the market even wants what they have to offer—and at what price. From there we look at internal operations, processes and work design, and then take up questions of hiring, new employee orientation, leadership, culture, and ethics, before offering our reflections and conclusions. We hope you enjoy the reading.

Chapter Two

EOC Companies:
Their Customers

There is only one valid definition of business purpose: to create a customer.[1]

Peter Drucker first offered the maxim noted above in his landmark 1974 book, *Management: Tasks, Responsibilities, Practices*,[2] and he offered it in very sharp contrast to what was then, and still is, a dominant understanding that the purpose of business is to maximize profit. Drucker dismissed the notion of profit making as purpose as not only false but also irrelevant and meaningless.[3] Drucker's point was that profit is not the motivation for business decisions and practices; rather, profitability is a test of how effective and therefore valid those business practices are. In characterizing the relevant purpose of any business as creating a customer, Drucker was contending that while profit is necessary, indeed crucial, a business is not really a business—a business, in fact, doesn't exist at all—until a customer is willing and able to purchase the product that the business offers. Business doesn't exist without a customer. This line of thinking leads Drucker to declare that each and every business enterprise has only two basic functions:

---

1. Drucker, Peter F. 2001. *The Essential Drucker: Selections from the Management Works of Peter F. Drucker.* HarperBusiness. New York: HarperCollins Publishers.
2. Drucker, Peter. 1974. *Management: Tasks, Responsibilities, and Practices.* New York: Harper & Row.
3. Drucker. *The Essential Drucker*, pp 18–19.

Those are, in his words, *marketing* and *innovation*.[4] So, in this chapter, we take up the question of *marketing* with our Economy of Communion companies.

Probably the best point at which to take up this discussion of marketing is with the distinction between *production-oriented* companies and *marketing-oriented* companies.[5] This distinction is clearly made in virtually every marketing textbook available because it is an important distinction, and because it has historically proven to matter a great deal.[6] The distinction can best be captured by considering the fundamental question of each orientation. A production-oriented company is one that is focused on its ability to produce and so is asking, "How might we sell that which we can make?" A marketing-oriented company is focused on what people want or need to buy and is asking, "How might we make that which we can sell?" In other words, a marketing orientation is focused on customers. Again, we can turn to Drucker:

> ... the aim of marketing is to make selling superfluous. The aim of marketing is to know and understand the customer so well that the product or service fits him and sells itself.[7]

We would argue that this focus and attention on customers is a fairly recent idea. One of the earliest milestones of this focus on customers might be the 1982 publication *In Search of Excellence*, the landmark study by Tom Peters and Bob Waterman.[8] Published at a time when U.S. industry was reeling from competitive challenges to our post-WWII

---

4. Ibid. p 20.
5. Levitt, Theodore. "Marketing Myopia." *Harvard Business Review*. 1975.
6. An exemplary example of how this has mattered is the U.S automotive industry in the late 1970s and early 1980s. U.S. automakers had been historically quite focused on production and quickly lost ground to Japanese automakers who were more focused on customer needs and wants. Among other places, this is documented in David Halberstam's 1986 work, *The Reckoning*.
7. Drucker. *The Essential Drucker.* p. 21.
8. Peters, Thomas J. and Waterman, Robert H. 1982. *In Search of Excellence*. Harper & Row, USA.

commercial and industrial hegemony—a period Peters and Waterman described as "our corporate malaise"[9]—the book was the outcome of several years of their research into what business practices accounted for excellence among American companies. One of their findings was as almost maniacal obsession with—you guessed it—customers. Since Peters and Waterman "discovered" this in their research, we cannot say they invented marketing orientation, but their work went a long way toward helping us understand and appreciate what Drucker was saying about customers and what smart companies—from all countries, in all industries—have been paying attention to ever since.

Peters and Waterman open their chapter on customers with a quotation from Lew Young, then editor in chief of *Business Week*. The essence of Young's comment is that despite what appears to be a *cultural*[10] emphasis on getting and remaining close to customers, the reality is that customers are either ignored or dismissed.[11] Young's comments suggest dissonance between company aspirations and actions. Companies may "understand" the importance of customer focus, but production-oriented habits, pressures to reduce short-term costs, and ignorance or lack of imagination can constrain the realization of that understanding. In other words, customer focus can often be more aspirational than actual.

Or customer focus can be intentionally non-existent. A research report published by the Pew Charitable Trust in 2001, *Aggravating Circumstances: A Status Report on Rudeness in America*, makes this point. While the project examined rudeness in all aspects of American life—from prejudice to road rage—one of the crucial findings concerned American consumers and their perceived treatment

---

9. Peters and Waterman. From the Introduction.
10. The italicized emphasis is ours and alludes to a broad understanding in the general business environment.
11. Peters and Waterman. p 156.

by businesses. According to the report, 46 percent of respondents indicated they had, in the previous year, walked out of a store for no other reason than rude treatment.[12] The report goes on to attribute much of the rudeness to poorly trained employees. However, Emily Yellin, in her book *Your Call is (Not That) Important to Us*, documents cases where rude, disrespectful, and degrading behavior on the part of employees toward customers—particularly over the phone in customer service environments—is an intentional, and possibly formal, corporate practice.[13]

Nevertheless, crucial attention to customers forms a large part of our current consciousness about what makes a company successful, excellent, good or great. So, if we want to understand the business practices of Economy of Communion companies in North America, we certainly want to know how they navigate these waters. Given the importance the EOC places on relationships and the primacy of their belief of putting the person at the center of the enterprise, it seems especially reasonable to wonder how EOC companies relate to their customers.

Thus, to borrow Drucker's words, how does a company create a customer? If a company were to take a strictly linear approach it would begin this process by conducting research to ascertain what is valuable and important to customers. The next step in this linear progression would be to ensure that the design and provision of a product or service "delivers" that value and importance. Finally, several other activities best described as promotion would follow.

However, we know empirically that these activities are, in fact, not linear but circular and so complex and deeply interconnected as to be difficult to distinguish. Moreover,

---

12. *Aggravating Circumstances: A Status Report on Rudeness in America.* Pew Charitable Trust. Public Agenda. 2001. (http://www.publicagenda.org/files/pdf/aggravating_circumstances.pdf)

13. Yellin, Emily. 2009. *Your Call is (Not That) Important to Us: Customer Service and What It Reveals About Our World and Our Lives.* Free Press. New York.

some would argue that customers do not always know what they want or what they value until they can see, hear, touch, taste, or smell a product.[14] This puts a business owner in the position of bringing his or her own insight and intuition to this process. Indeed, there is some history of products being developed to solve problems experienced by a business owner, who then discovers that other people are looking for such a solution.[15] Despite the admitted limitations of a linear approach, it serves as a handy organizational structure for presenting what we learned from our EOC companies. What follows are separate sections detailing the practices of (1) understanding customers (market research), (2) translating those understandings into products for those customers (product development), and then (3) promoting those products in some fashion (promotion). Under the label of promotion, we will consider two basic activities; first, the activities aimed at informing both existing and potential customers, i.e., advertising and the like, and second, activities devoted to creating some sort of identity for the company, for the product, or for both that are most appropriately labeled "branding," Let's begin by examining how our companies have used market research and in what type of research have they engaged.

Marketing Research: Learning about Customers

Despite their variation in size, type of business, geographic location and geographic scope, nine of the companies report their marketing research activity in a manner that can best be described as *listening*. For many of these companies, this type of listening is the only research they do or have done. Some, like La Parola, claim to do no research but

---

14. Probably the most reliable source for this sentiment is Steve Jobs, former CEO of Apple. In a May 25, 1998, article in *Business Week*, by Sager and Burrows, he argues, "It's really hard to design products by focus groups. A lot of times, people don't know what they want until you show it to them."
15. Von Hippel, Eric. 1994. *The Sources of Innovation*. Oxford University Press: USA.

to simply engage their customers in ongoing conversation, which certainly must be a straightforward practice for a language academy. Finish Line listens to parents and students every day, while Sofia gets routine and valuable feedback from their dealers and from the musicians who own their instruments. Others extend their listening to not only possible or potential customers but also various experts, other experienced business people, family, friends, and, in some cases, possible future competitors. For example, initial market research for Terra Nuova amounted to conversations with three people; an old friend, an antique dealer, and a master restorer. Similarly, Spiritours' first product, the trip to Santiago de Compostela, grew out of conversations with friends and family, in particular a French actor who was popularizing the pilgrimage.

Beyond listening in this way, several companies also invested in other forms of market research. In addition to conversations with customers, First Fruits also subscribes to industry periodicals and maintains membership in agriculture-related organizations. Ideal reports interviewing business contacts in similar or related businesses using a prepared set of questions. In addition, Ideal conducts Internet research, reads trade magazines, and sifts through trade association websites in order to learn more about the industry and the marketplace. Ideal also consulted with local economic development agencies. CHB conducted online research via the LinkedIn social network (a way of "trolling for prospects"), and used focus groups in the local market area. They also belong to the Professional Business Coach Alliance. Netuitive may have the most systematic and sophisticated approach, relying on interviews and surveys with potential customers and market leaders, including large Fortune 100 companies, as well as conversations with leading industry analysts such as Gartner, EMA, and Forrester. Netuitive also benchmarks existing successful approaches and has established an advisory board made up of their long-term customers.

Some of our company owners and executives also validate the notion of bringing their own insight and intuition to this activity, an approach we would label *listening to experience*. As mentioned, Spiritours certainly engages in conversations with customers, but at least one offering, the safari in Kenya, grew out of the owners' profound personal experience in that country and her subsequent desire for others to share in that experience. Mundell & Associates simply reports the sum of their marketing research as the owners' 30 years of experience in the business. (We would also note that these years of experience are backed up by impressive technical expertise in a number of related sciences, but more about that later).

One of the more interesting answers to this whole question comes from Arc-en-Saisons. The owner devotes almost no time and energy to the "demand" side of the business but rather focuses on "supply," which is to say, in his case, becoming the best provider. He has not done market research, but he does do "operational" research, i.e., searching for ways to better accomplish the work. Much of this is trial and error. He maintains that there is a best way to accomplish routine tasks and cites window washing as an example: There is really a correct way to wash windows effectively and efficiently. The owner claims that he learned this method by trial and error and that not many people — even people who wash windows for a living — know this proper and best technique. To these ends, the owner is very inquisitive about best practices and best tools; thus, he is always interested in learning something from any supplier about new products for maintenance.

Perhaps the best illustration of these multiple approaches to market research — that is, *listening* to customers and *listening to experience* — comes from Dealerflow. Here's what they had to say:

We relied primarily on personal experience and discussions and observations working in large and small companies, in the information technology (IT) field; did a lot of reading and attending conferences in the HR software space to come up to speed on that; read a lot of blogs, online and printed articles in the areas of consumer software (Facebook, Twitter, Google Docs, Gmail/Gtalk, etc.), enterprise software, HR software, software business models, and vertical software in the auto dealership space. We don't do a lot of formal research because it is hard to find something timely and relevant and when you do it's expensive. We do read research reports by the likes of Gartner, IDC, Forrester, etc, but they are usually behind the curve. I love to talk directly to customers, but it's difficult to find value in it until we have a product or at least a prototype or something to show them so that they can react, otherwise we are asking them to envision something that is difficult for them. It's like asking someone if they would like a steak marinated a certain way, and then cooked a certain way. But if you have the prepared steak and give them a bite, they can tell you if they like it.[16]

Continuing in our linear discussion, the next topic is how to translate input from market research into products, goods and/or services that customers need or want and are willing to purchase. We will refer to this process simply as product development.

Product Development

It is not our intent here to review each of the companies one by one with a recitation of their products (we would refer readers back to Chapter One for this) but rather to focus our attention on the noteworthy dimensions of their products that illustrate their practice and approach to being mindful of their customers. One of the striking features of most, if not all, of these EOC companies, is that their

---

16. From Survey 3, February 2009.

goods and services occupy a unique niche in the market-place, offer some unique benefit, or possess some unique characteristics. When specifically asked about products and services and their unique value, every one of these companies is able to identify and discuss some form of unique advantage. We would argue that this reflects a noteworthy translation of what they know and understand about their customers. The factors that contribute to uniqueness are considerably varied from one company to the next, ranging from the nearly common, like naturally raised farm live-stock (First Fruits), to the singularly sublime, like patented and proprietary algorithms (Netuitive). But even First Fruits enhances what they offer customers by selling the naturally raised livestock, poultry and eggs directly to customers, who can, in effect, hand-pick their purchases.

Terra Nuova offers a ceramic restoration of such high quality as to be nearly undetectable; in fact, the company must caution its customers to label the product as restored rather than original. Terra Nuova describes its unique value for the customer as a combination of a fair price for services and the restored value of items. Finish Line recognizes that tutoring a student is really a family affair, that student success requires a support network, and that their customer is in a sense the student *and* the family. Arc-en-Saisons and CHB, who serve two vastly different sets of customers, nevertheless are alike in offering completely individualized services with Arc-en-Saisons offering complete customization. Everything is tailored to a specific customer's needs. La Parola has the insight to offer language training not in a classroom but by engaging with students in everyday activities, such as hiking and cooking. La Parola believes language is not an abstract thing to be learned but a means of everyday communication that must be used. Ideal has realized that for training employees whose native language is Spanish, there is no better way to teach critical skills involving health and safety than by teaching in two languages.

Here are four more extended examples of how these
EOC companies have translated their market research into
distinctive offerings:

1. Spiritours offers 25 different tours, among them
   four of which seem to be most popular: a pilgrimage to Santiago de Compostela; Morocco; Egypt and
   Mount Sinai; and a pilgrimage to the Holy Land.
   In describing these tours, Spiritours uses spiritual
   language and, by calling particular tours "pilgrimages," signals their explicitly spiritual purpose. Descriptions suggest an emphasis on spirituality, unity,
   love, intercultural experiences, and sharing, and
   sometimes include direct interaction with Focolare
   communities.[17] Spiritours describes tours in which
   travelers experience tranquility and beauty both in
   nature and within themselves. The Santiago de Compostela tour, for example, is described as a "step-
   by-step journey by foot... a test of physical, mental
   and spiritual endurance. It complements the internal
   journey that helps people get to know themselves
   better and, at the end, to feel a little more serenity
   and peace."[18] Another tour description has travelers
   participating in "workshops on personal balance,
   the spirituality of unity, and local inculturation." A
   safari with a "spiritual dimension to it" includes two
   nights in a permanent Mariapolis[19] where travelers
   "learn about the spirituality of unity, the art of loving
   and inculturation" and then are encouraged to put
   their learning into practice during the safari. When
   tours include visits to schools, hospitals, and so on,
   travelers are encouraged to bring materials to share.

17. There is a Focolare community, for example, in Nairobi which is a vital stop during
    the tour to Kenya.
18. From interviews.
19. Mariapolis is the Focolare term used to describe their communities. The meaning is
    "City of Mary."

Cultivating relationships based on trust with locals allows Spiritours to take travelers into the Sahara. Pilgrims to the Holy Land read the Gospel passages associated with sites visited, and they are invited to "meditate in silence in these sacred places."

2. Mundell & Associates identifies five services: environmental consulting; geophysical surveys; human health risk assessments; water resources consulting; and permitting/regulatory support. Mundell & Associates describes each in terms that emphasize the firm's technical capabilities, its experience, and its scientific and engineering knowledge. There is no language here to suggest the unique value of services in terms of EOC values, which, of course, is not to say that there are none.

3. Netuitive's product is self-learning performance management software that replaces human guesswork with automated mathematics and analysis to understand normal system behavior across IT silos, to isolate root causes, and to forecast problems for mission-critical applications. Netuitive's software is based on multi-patented algorithmic research that provides unprecedented levels of automation. Netuitive describes its products using strictly technical language.

4. Sofia makes and sells violins of premium quality, which the owner suggests provides the products' "sizzle." Products are handmade, "carefully crafted reproductions of various early Italian instruments."[20] Unique patina and sound adjusted by computer provide added value, as does an unlimited warranty for each instrument.

---

20. From interviews.

Here let us pause to reiterate that the linear approach we have adopted as an outline for presenting our findings does not quite capture the extent of the true, ongoing interaction between the practice of listening to customers and to one's own intuition (market research) and the process of developing, changing, reinventing, and refining what is offered (product development). Nevertheless, we continue, and the next logical topic in our progression is *promotion*. Given the extent to which many of these EOC companies can point to a uniquely valuable product or service, how do they make others aware of what they have to offer? How do they continue to communicate with past and current customers?

Promotion

Arguably, there is a level of detail that must be attended to with respect to promotion. The importance of such things as word-of-mouth promotion, referrals, and cultivating pre-sale relationships must be somewhat a function of competitive dynamics and somewhat a function of the type of product offering (i.e., some goods and services are better served by different forms of promotion). But sales messages (well-polished or not), websites, online messaging, and, in particular, paid advertising and promotional brochures all require specific intention. A marketing message must be carefully considered, developed, and polished, and the decision to use certain media, approaches or distribution outlets is an intentional one. The owners of EOC companies must make these decisions just as other business owners do. Even the decision not to say certain things (or to say anything at all) is an intentional one.

Intriguing insights can be gleaned from the decisions that EOC business owners make with regard to promotion. We explored the details of their marketing, communications, and, in particular, their approach to advertising and branding. We were interested in specific ways that EOC businesses might be communicating with their customers and wanted to deepen our understanding of how they think about these vital and common business practices. Advertising is one business practice that can be very revealing about a company's values and sense of itself. As consumers, we generally place a significant value on "truth' in advertising and are very sensitive, and perhaps skeptical, of advertising claims. We are on guard against the powerful and sometimes negative effects of advertising that depends heavily on psychology to turn wants into needs or that promotes consumerism and otherwise shapes our behavior.[21] At the same time, we are hungry for information about the products and services we consume and about the companies that offer them. Indeed this is precisely the view of advertising prevalent in economics.

Clearly then, advertising and communication practices can reveal much about a company and so it is perhaps fitting that we begin our examination of EOC business practices here. Questions we might ask are, how is the spirituality of unity expressed when EOC companies communicate with their customers? Moreover, how do EOC business owners even think about it? How important is it to them? How much time and effort do they invest in it? How do they conceive of "success" in this arena? What causes them to change their communication strategy?

Advertising and Communication

Perhaps it should be no surprise that the dominant approach to promotion for these companies is word of mouth, which underscores the importance of *reputation* and *relationships*. To be sure, the reliance on word-of-mouth promotion is dictated for some of these companies by the nature of their industry, their particular geographic location, or the

---

21. Schor, Juliet. 2004. *Born to Buy: The Commercialized Child and the New Consumer Culture*. New York: Scribners.

nature of their goods or services. Netuitive, for example, recognizes that "In metropolitan areas, the top IT leaders know one another and validate their vendors' selection among themselves."[22] Consequently, word-of-mouth promotion is very important to the company, accounting for 10 to 20 percent of their new sales annually. Terra Nuova estimates that word-of-mouth promotion accounts for almost 95 percent of its revenue. More than half of Spiritours' business stems from word-of-mouth promotions.[23] For these companies, word-of-mouth promotion is an intentional strategy. It receives specific management attention as an advertising practice.

But for others, word-of-mouth promotion is a byproduct of their conviction to be intentional about relationships. Mundell & Associates, for example, aims to satisfy one client at a time (living the present moment) and thereby establish a relationship. Paying attention to the relationship with each customer will eventually generate referrals from satisfied customers.[24] Finish Line places tremendous importance on word-of mouth. According to the principal here, "Tutoring is a word-of-mouth business primarily; once you have a reputation, it spreads; because we have an intangible service, we are VERY particular about our reputation — it's really all we have."[25] For these companies, reputation becomes a marketing objective — an intentional objective they are willing to strive for. They are all very particular about their reputations and proactively invest in protecting and nurturing those reputations. For these companies, specific management attention is paid first and foremost to relationships. Referrals come from satisfied customers and from other businesses and community entities with which their companies have cultivated solid relationships.

---

22. From Survey 4, April 2009.
23. From Field Study Interviews, June 2010.
24. From Survey 4, April 2009.
25. From Field Study Interviews, June 2010.

Mundell & Associates is quite sophisticated in this regard. Most of the company's referrals come from individuals who have had satisfactory experiences with Mundell & Associates; only a few customers come as referrals through other businesses, but one of those customers was the State of Indiana, one of the company's largest clients. Focusing on repeat business is a main focus. "Keeping and developing relationships that last is probably the thing we do the best, and is in line with the EOC,"[26] Building customer relationships before a sale is important, and Mundell & Associates regularly devotes time and energy to this, getting to know potential customers by taking them to lunch, listening to their problems, and trying to focus on small areas where the company may offer a good fit.

Netuitive can point to some singular achievement with respect to relationship building. Netuitive has a "100% maintenance renewal (customer satisfaction rate) that is very rare in the industry,"[27] and says that customer referrals represent "the most effective promotion for our business of all."[28] Although referrals from other businesses are not the industry norm, Netuitive was recently "invited by one of the larger companies in our industry (HP Software) to join their by-invitation only referral program where their sales people can refer business to us when customers have a special need that only Netuitive can fulfill."[29] Netuitive is building its business model on repeat or "add-on" business, without which the company would not be profitable. "70% of our pipeline for the remainder of the year is repeat business with existing customers. This quarter the repeat business will account for 80% of the total turnover."

Building customer relationships before the sale is "crucial" for Netuitive. As a small business competing with

---

26. From Survey 4, April 2009.
27. Ibid.
28. Ibid.
29. Ibid..

much larger public companies, Netuitive can win only through technical superiority. As long as they have won a prospect's trust, Netuitive can deliver on its promises and accompany the growth of their customer's business. In the end, most customers say they ultimately selected Netuitive because they trusted the company and wanted a partner rather than "just buying technology." Netuitive instills trust in its customers that when things go wrong (and they will, because software is not an exact science), Netuitive will go beyond the call of duty to help make things right. Netuitive intentionally establishes multiple touch points at multiple levels of the prospect company — from the implementation technicians to the CEO — to establish that critical trust before the sale.

For Spiritours, referrals from other agencies have oc-curred in the past, but this is not a significant source of business for the company. About five percent of Spiritours' customers have already done at least two tours in the past; some have taken as many as seven prior tours (and the company has only been in business five-and-a-half years). The company also gets repeat business from big organiza-tions like the Archdiocese of Montreal, which entrusts to Spiritours the youth business associated with World Youth Day, which is held every two to three years. Spiritours' advertising in specialized magazines generates some busi-ness, but the company relies more heavily on promotional brochures — distributing 60,000 flyers and 3,500 brochures each year — in an effort to build customer relationships before the sale.

Seventy-five percent of Terra Nuova's customers are re-ferred by other satisfied customers and another five percent come from other business referrals. About 85 percent of an-nual revenues are generated in repeat business. Terra Nuova invests heavily in building customer relationships before the sale. The owner says that before a sale he has a conversation with every customer; about half of these conversations are conducted on the phone, half in person. "Items are given over to me only after a conversation. My address is not published (on purpose), so we must first build this customer relationship and thoroughly understand our expectations." Terra Nuova uses direct mail (letters) to connect with past customers. According to the owner, "This month I sent 20 personal letters to old customers who haven't used me in about 6 months... the letter offered understanding and empathy for the hurting economy, and offered an appealing reduction in my estimates to help fill in my backlog this quarter. After one week, nine (customers) responded with work."[30] He adds: "New prospects (walk-ins or potential customers I first meet) always want to see examples of my workmanship. I carry a small box of two restored items and pictures of their 'before.' That, plus name-dropping another customer who uses me, is enough to make them trust."[31]

The owner of CHB says "it's all about relationships." He cites CHB's membership in the local chamber of commerce and in Business Network International (BNI) as crucial pieces of the company's efforts to pick up referrals. He solicits testimonies from satisfied customers to use in his marketing. He characterized both the website and the brochures as necessities, but not for generating business in and of themselves. He says generating business requires the relationships, referrals, and testimonials.

Only two of our EOC companies use any kind of <u>paid advertising</u>. Mundell & Associates has been an underwriter for National Public Radio (NPR) almost since the start of the company, and Spiritours has purchased advertising in specialized magazines from time to time. While Mundell & Associates believes that their advertising has generated considerable business for them over the years, Spiritours really relies more on other means to bring in business. Finish

---

30. From Field Study Interviews, June 2010.
31. Ibid.

Line does no paid advertising at all (and hasn't for 10 years). The company does visit schools to drop off business cards or touch base, and it has materials requested by schools for upcoming SAT workshops. Netuitive uses no promotional brochures and no paid advertising, relying instead on Internet and direct marketing. Partly because of its specialized niche market, Netuitive reaches prospects with direct marketing initiatives (mail, email, Internet, and specialized seminars or conferences). Although some companies in its industry advertise, Netuitive sees that "as brand promotion and in some cases 'ego-marketing.'" Thus, in effect, paid advertising is an approach to communicating with customers that is not broadly pursued by these EOC companies.

Neither is Internet marketing. Only Mundell & Associates, Netuitive, Spiritours, and Terra Nuova report their websites to be an important driver of business, and Terra Nuova sees only about five percent of its business generated in this fashion. These four, plus First Fruits and CHB are the six companies that utilize any internet presence. The remaining companies do not utilize the internet at all.

Branding and Identity

The notion of branding—developing a brand and building a brand image—is typically a very demanding and very expensive undertaking for companies, and we have no wish to portray any of these EOC companies as intent on becoming recognizable brand names on a world-wide basis. However, there is an element of developing an identity and a consistency across marketing approaches that small businesses and even sole-proprietorships recognize as worthwhile and valuable. These EOC companies are no different. Here's what they have said about that.

Spiritours reports that their central message is about offering soulful journeys, or as their name and logo suggest, spiritual tours. Their slogan is "Open your eyes, your heart and your mind to the inner and the outer worlds." The marketing message here is grounded in what appears to be a genuine belief that travel is good for people. In the owner's words, people can not only learn and discover other cultures through traveling, but also open their minds, contemplate beauty, and grow spiritually. Spiritours' materials and website use inspiring pictures in order to convey a sense of peacefulness, harmony, and beauty. That message seems to attract people in search of such an experience, so the message appears to be well understood.

Spiritours is fairly sophisticated in its use of communication and promotion methods. The owner does some of the creative work for promotions herself, but turns this work over to graphic design professionals for completion. The company has been the subject of some good magazine stories, and the owner seems to be a good interview subject. Googling Spiritours brings up all kinds of spirit-related sites, but Spiritours is right there at the top of the page. The website is attractive and easy to use. What is really unique about Spiritours is their use of YouTube videos to showcase various trips and to use the kind of photos that might have great appeal to someone thinking about an adventure. The EOC connection is not a part of these videos.

La Parola wants to convey to students that they—the students—are the center of the owner's life and that they are more important to her than herself. The owner claims to do this in writing and in practice but it's not clear how the owner actually makes connection with potential customers. The very personal approach she takes in teaching Italian is quite interesting but is certainly nothing that could be conveyed on a business card. La Parola has no website "yet," leaving the impression that there may be one in the future.

Finish Line does no advertising in the open market. Most of their business is word-of-mouth, so their success breeds additional success. At one point, however, Finish Line did use an ad agency (but one related to the founder of Finish Line) that helped them "tremendously."

The fact that Finish Line has no website is interesting because most high school students—and their parents—would start with the web in searching for a tutor. In any case, when the owner says the company depends on word-of-mouth advertising, she means it, because other than business cards, Finish Line has done little or no promotional communication for about seven years.

First Fruits conveys its central message by word-of-mouth also, and that message revolves around quality of livestock at a fair price. The owner reports that many of her customers can be resellers (that is, someone buying from First Fruits in order to resell to consumers), and these resellers typically complain that other producers charge prices that are too high. Googling First Fruits brings up lots of businesses, but not this one. The limited communications methods that First Fruits uses all seem to focus on the local market, which is understandable but also curious. If the business is promoting free-range chickens, why not promote the business where young, health-conscious users are likely to look first? She makes no mention of working directly with coops or advertising in coops or neighborhood papers. Perhaps this is one of those businesses that is truly an extension of the owner's lifestyle or her avocation. In any case, First Fruits makes use of only a few, very limited methods for promoting its products.

Mundell & Associates is trying to communicate that it is highly technical, very competent, and well qualified in its specialties; passionate about cleaning up the earth; and passionate about solving difficult problems. The company does have a reputation for helping with the most difficult environmental problems. The owner indicates that, for the most part, he has forged this reputation on his own, without really seeking advice from others, but now, as he has added employees over the past 14 years, these employees "have had increasing input as to the message and what we say." He indicates he wants to increase this input even more, especially as his employees begin to understand the EOC. He believes the company's message has been consistent, and that the only measure of its effectiveness is their growth and what people have said to them directly. For example, the company has received one community award and he is regularly told that "people hear good things" about the company. Mundell & Associates uses multiple communications methods, and the description of each and how they are used reveals a certain sophistication or, at the very least, a well-considered plan for what part each contributes to Mundell & Associates' overall marketing message.

Of all the companies in the study, Mundell & Associates has gone the farthest in advertising and promotion, using both print and broadcast formats, but choosing selectively in the broadcast arena to focus on public radio and TV. The owner reports that the efforts have had a strong impact on the company's visibility in the community, but he does not say whether he thinks it has affected business. Mundell & Associates stands with Spiritours in most effectively communicating the EOC connection. Googling Mundell & Associates quickly gets one to the company website, which provides ample information about the business philosophy, its EOC connection, and the nature and capacity of its consulting business.

Sofia introduced their violins with a full-page ad containing endorsements from concertmasters of the Chicago Symphony Orchestra and the Henry Mancini Orchestra. They have always sold "quality," defined as "striking in beauty of sound and appearance," a positioning which was unique in the industry at the time the company started.[32] Sofia seems to have a good sense for the impact of choosing and using a good variety of marketing communications and

---

32. From Survey 4, April 2009.

promotion methods. The company has a brand name and logo which are recognized widely by potential customers, i.e., serious musicians.

Perhaps Sofia's unique approach is seeking product endorsement from famous musicians. The company uses dealers around the world, so perhaps the ability of the individual dealers also play a significant role in their communications strategy. Although Sofia does have a website, it is very basic, offering product and dealer information, but no pricing data, no demonstrations, no "glitz." Sofia's web presence misses the chance for impact. For example, though famous musicians endorse the company's violins, the website makes no mention of this. Googling the company by name immediately brings up the website, but it also brings up a blog in which potential users critique Sofia, and the input is mixed. There is no mention of the EOC on its web page.

CHB focuses its message on working with business owners and executives to help them identify and achieve their goals. The company places high emphasis on its value-centered approach—EOC values—and the role of these values in providing clarity to clients as they "assess their situation, refine their strategy and ...execute their plan."[33] The owner of CHB is very intentional about developing and maintaining congruence between his marketing message, the social teaching of the Church, and the EOC philosophy and feels it (the emphasis on these values and this congruence) is a very effective approach. At the same time he avoids any proselytizing or "preachiness" and believes his ability to convey this message in that particular manner has improved over time and with experience. The fundamental message, however, remains unchanged. CHB does use a logo for an image of clarity and guidance, and their tagline is "Progressive approach to results; no quick fix." The company has no trademarked emblem but it does have letter-

---

33. From Survey 4, April 2009.

head and business cards. CHB conveys its message mostly over its website and through social media, reinforced with some advertisements and brochures. The company uses no broadcast commercials or telemarketing and has no written customer policies, warranties, guarantees or promises. CHB is a direct-selling operation.

While Terra Nuova makes limited use of marketing and promotion methods, the owner does seem to have a good command of the word-of-mouth approach as well as the endorsement approach. The Terra Nuova website, which is simple, is nonetheless interesting, offering examples of successful work the company has done and identifying antique dealers who recommend the service. The owner has had favorable publicity in two magazines. Because the company appears to depend heavily on its website, it is worth noting that one has to be looking for Terra Nuova to find the website. Googling ceramics repair or Delft china repair does not lead you to the Terra Nuova website, and once on the site, there is no mention of EOC.

Arc-en-Saisons does have a rainbow logo, but it is not trademarked and only appears on the owner's business card, which, as it turns out, is the only promotional material the company has.

Summary Observations

It might prove helpful here to reflect on what these companies have to say. First of all being a part of the EOC is not "magical"; it does not afford a company any surefire, new or different approach to marketing. In fact, participation in the EOC presents some challenges to these business owners. Mundell & Associates even mentions this in a response to a question about repeat business being the result of building relationships. He describes the challenge as determining which marketing approaches are "in line with EOC...." So, what we mean about not magical is that each business owner has to determine what business practice is both good for business AND "in line with the EOC," and being "in line" is not a question of following the letter of the law, but the spirit. Each business owner has to be conscientious and intentional in what he or she does.

Another general thought is that many of these businesses have a uniqueness — a product differentiation advantage, a niche advantage, or both. Mundell & Associates has specialized expertise; Netuitive is in a specialized niche; Sofia has a specialized niche (the best factory- produced violin); Spiritours offers the "retreat aspect — the silence, the walking pilgrimages" and a particular "openness to opportunity; Terra Nuova offers a unique niche restoration service; and Finish Line seems to embody the principle of focusing on customers and not on their competitors.

One can hardly overstate the pivotal importance of word of mouth, reputation, and relationship marketing in these EOC companies: It is one thing they all have in common and something in which they all take pride. It is interesting that having a well-crafted message to deliver is not equally important. Perhaps the power of word-of-mouth marketing is not so much about details — pricing, quality of work, capability, flexibility and turnaround — as it is about trust and the appeal of the character of people and the organization itself. Word of mouth, though obviously effective, also poses significant risk, does it not? One bad experience, one verbal and aggressively unhappy customer could potentially do a lot of harm. It also appears that the companies rely more and more on web technologies to get their message out. Several have all but given up on brochures.

Of all the companies, Spiritours is most explicit in offering a product whose unique value is connected with EOC values and philosophy. The concern for customers in the delivery of services that is expressed by Finish Line and La Parola also has obvious connections to EOC values, but their expression is not as overt as that of Spiritours. Dealerflow also speaks to some extent about a product that facilitates unity in the corporate environment.

The companies vary significantly in their use of communications methods for marketing and promotion. None appears to have a marketing person whose work is dedicated to this cause, nor does there seem to be a pattern of approaches. However, the businesses do tend to sort themselves out on a continuum from the simplest of approaches (business cards and letterhead) to the more complex (websites and YouTube videos). The larger companies, of course, are the ones who make the most use of the various communication technologies and who also seem to have a good grasp of the need for a strong, clear message. It's interesting that these companies, in general, are quite modest in staking their claims as EOC businesses. Mundell & Associates and Spiritours go farthest here. But, surprisingly, some of the companies make no mention of EOC at all.

The limited use of web technology is also surprising. Using a Google search turned up the various web pages only when the firm's name actually appeared in the search terms. For example, "environmental consultant" did not take us to Mundell & Associates; and "Delft china repair" did not take us to Terra Nuova. Finally, all the data here point to both the necessity and the centrality of reliance on word-of-mouth advertising, which suggests that the companies, as a whole, either do not have a good grasp of marketing communications and promotion or they do not have the money or the will to use other methods more skillfully.

Any research project surfaces questions that should have been asked but were not or that, in retrospect, would have been useful questions to ask. In this arena of *creating and keeping customers*, here's our short list. 1) Do you think your product or service is in any way influenced by the fact that your business is an EOC company? 2) If your business were not influenced by EOC, would that change anything about your service or your products? 3) Where do you see the EOC "value added" coming into the picture with regard to your service or product? But, at least, in a subsequent chapter we will explore their marketing communication, pricing, and sales practices in a bit more depth.

Chapter Three

EOC Companies:
Competitive Practices
and Pricing

I n the previous chapter, we observed that each of these
companies has the ability to articulate a unique product
or service advantage. This seemed noteworthy to us for
two reasons. One, since each of the owners was able to recognize and articulate this, it suggests that the importance
of such an advantage is quite apparent to them, and two,
because such advantage was intentional and not accidental.
And so, among these owners there is a particular awareness
or consciousness about competition that seems particularly
business savvy. This was evidence of a noteworthy level
or quality of insight that, while not rare, may not be com-
monplace either.

When we started to organize, summarize, and present
material on competitive behavior, the responses received
to a question we had asked about critical success factors
offered us an intriguing place to start. For again, the level
of business savvy and insight seemed noteworthy. Perhaps
equally noteworthy is that we believed we needed to ask
these owners to specifically consider what made their companies successful — apart from divine providence. In other
words, had we simply asked what made their company successful, each owner would have immediately, easily, and
naturally, credited such providence, and, would have been
able to offer story after story as evidence. (And we will
recount some of those stories in a later chapter.) But we

wanted to learn specifically how and in what ways these business owners connected certain concrete business or management practices with success in a competitive arena; hence, the specificity of our question.

Success is not conceived as 'winning" at competition, but rather as "sustainability" in the most current and popular expression of that idea. What can't be overstated is the extent to which the answer to this question of critical success factors across all of the companies is that it is their understanding of their business as primarily a *set of relationships* that makes them successful. Let us explain further. We observe that it is common parlance in management circles these days to make statements like, "our employees are our greatest assets," or "We put our customers first." Statements like these would lead one to believe that certainly, it must be common wisdom in business that relationships are important and must be attended to. Regardless of whether that is actually true or not, we find that EOC businesses view things a bit differently.

To these business owners, the business is, before and above all else, a set of relationships. When asked about success it's not just that they nurture this set of relationships; it's that their *view* of the business as a set of relationships becomes an "intangible asset"—in the words of one business owner—that has positive and concrete effects both economic and financial. These owners know this and point it out. It's more than a warm, fuzzy, feeling, or a socially legitimate[1] way to talk about customers or employees. It's a real competitive advantage.

Here's the way they describe this at Netuitive:

> The integrity, the ingenuity, the level of dedication, the sense of responsibility, the mutual respect, the belief in win-win situations, the openness to work across boundaries, the customer service orientation, the preference for long term

---

1. This is legitimacy as posited by DiMaggio and Powell, 1983

solutions and for doing the "right thing" for our employees...
is something truly special.[2]

And at Mundell & Associates:

People tend to find "something more" when they work with
us and, all things being equal, will choose to work with us
again because of that intangible asset we bring. Of course,
many years of experience dealing with tough problems,
good educational backgrounds, and the ability to communicate with both common people and very technically-minded
people are also key assets. So, we could say: past successes,
quality-driven, people-oriented, good communicators—are
key to our success.[3]

Other of our companies invoke the Golden Rule as a way
of describing this. First Fruits mentions treating suppliers as
they would like to be treated. Sofia Violins and Finish Line
both, in fact, specifically use the term "Golden Rule." Others specifically mention relationships. CHB frames much
of their response in terms of "relationship capital." Finish
Line talks about "reciprocal relationships." Spiritours specifically identifies "relationships" and "choosing the right
people to work with" as success factors. They also point out
that clients and Finish Line together have all become like
family. As usual, the most straightforward response here is
provided by La Parola, who simply says that she loves her
students and that they know she goes out of her way to love
them.

For these companies, though, success is not just about
this intangible. There is also a recognition of, appreciation
for, and focus on elements of product or service *quality*. The
evidence that they recognize and appreciate an idea about
quality is embedded in many of the comments. Netuitive
mentions their customer service orientation, their ingenuity
and their dedication. Finish Line realizes that customers

2. From Survey 10, December 2009.
3. Ibid.

know they care and that they are always there in "every way possible" for them. Everyone who calls Finish Line or comes in realizes that their needs are perceived as important. Mundell & Associates points out that part of their vision is a very high priority on quality. Sofia Violins mentions product quality again and again as their crucial distinction. Spiritours identifies "giving...great service" and planning that eliminates or minimizes asking the client to assume any risk.

In some ways, these comments leave us with a timeless and therefore somewhat chronic question about the precise or operational definition of quality. Perhaps "timeless' and "chronic" are too strong a choice of words, but if we were to examine commonly accepted management ideas and practices going back to the late 1970's and early 1980's through certainly the late 1990's, this was a serious question. What do we mean by *quality*? It was a question made more serious by the quality revolution of Deming and Juran that was occurring at that time, and the obvious manufacturing prowess evident in goods manufactured outside the U.S.; most notably automobiles manufactured in Japan. What began back then evolved through other gurus like Philip Crosby and Michael Hammer, through statistical process control (SPC) and quality circles to a widespread adoption of lean enterprise principles and six-sigma black belt programs.

And so we know that the best management thinking these days recognizes that quality must be precisely defined so that it can then be knowingly and intentionally delivered. Regrettably, we were not able to wrest any such precise definition from our EOC business owners. At the same time, there is an inescapable and largely intuitive sense that what they mean by quality is certainly *unwavering and uncompromised reliability*. This is evident in the responses from Sofia Violins, Netuitive, Mundell & Associates, and Spiritours. They also mean consistency of product, customer delight, and an acute sense of excellence.

But there is more. These business owners, often as a way of trying to summarize their own individual musings on this question come back to an idea that can only be described as a "gestalt"; that given their approach to business, every encounter with them is a very special and unique encounter and it is this gestalt that really sets them apart. Let's look at an additional comment from Netuitive and revisit the comment above from Mundell & Associates. First Netuitive:

> I believe that **our collaborative and open culture is truly a competitive differentiator**... It helps get the best out of us and our customers and partners. The levels of productivity exceed the mere addition of people. When we make positive choices that sometimes involve an act of faith to do the right thing (because the mere economics may tell us otherwise) we often experience unexpected 'gifts' in form of unexpected/ creative ideas, new business, great hires or financing during a credit crunch.[4]

Two things deserve comment here. First is the recognition that levels of productivity expand beyond just the numbers or addition of people. There is a concrete advantage that is greater than mere headcount. Second is that economic factors are not the only consideration in good decision making because they can't account for all possible benefits. Now to return to Mundell & Associates:

> People tend to find "something more" when they work with us and, all things being equal, will choose to work with us again because of that intangible asset we bring. Of course, many years of experience dealing with tough problems, good educational backgrounds, and the ability to communicate with both common people and very technically-minded people are also key assets. So, we could say: past successes, quality-driven, people-oriented, good communicators — are key to our success.[5]

---

4. From Survey 10, December 2009.
5. Ibid.

Again, there is a gestalt here. There is "something more" than merely the additive effect of various elements or qualities or properties or practices of the company.

And finally, there is a wonderful recognition embedded in a comment from Sofia Violins that points to the source of this gestalt; the recognition that all of the challenges of owning a company, operating a business, and pursuing any kind of success in a competitive arena are tied to the practice of living in the present moment. This is not just an idealistic platitude, but a clear-eyed recognition that an EOC business owner must let go of yesterday's crises and failures as well as yesterday's successes and triumphs. This is a normative management lesson; yesterday cannot be undone. It can serve as a powerful teacher, but only today, and tomorrow, and a succession of tomorrows, are what matter.

The perspective of EOC business owners on what contributes to their success evidences a solid understanding of competition and competitive dynamics. At the same time that they recognize this perception of the business as a set of relationships, and recognize the intangible asset this provides them, they also recognize that it serves them well in the competitive arena. But, it's clear that they don't pursue the gestalt opportunistically or instrumentally. The most accurate way to describe this is to say they know no other way to conceive of their business and of no other way to nurture their attitude toward competition.

We can now turn our attention to specific business practices that are manifest in their approach and practice of competing. Specifically, we want to examine their approach to selling and their approach to pricing. In the previous chapter, we discussed marketing practices and indeed the lines of distinction between some of these practices are blurred and so it is difficult to decide when marketing stops and competing begins, for marketing activities themselves are a form of competition. Yet, we need some way to organize our data such that it is intelligible and relevant to practices that business people might recognize in their own business. To that end, we'll begin with an attempt to provide some context for this by investigating the sales process.

Selling and the Sales Process

Specifically, we are interested in the sales cycle. Again in the previous chapter we remarked on how important it is to these companies to build relationships with their customers prior to any sale. Here we are more interested in the "mechanics" of selling. And as we might expect, there is considerable variation, most of which seems driven by the type of product offered. And the responses of our companies here provide more information about the business and the products and/or services offered by the business and also help us to understand a bit more about the type, quality, and duration of the relationship with customers.

For three companies, selling is an immediate occurrence. Terra Nuova reports a very short sales cycle. According to the owner, decisions to purchase services (i.e., have a piece restored) are made almost "immediately after an estimate" is provided, and there is little to no comparison shopping since the service is "unique." And of course, given the importance of referrals and repeat business to his company, there is a predisposition to use the services at the time an estimate is requested. Finish Line and La Parola similarly report that sales occur on a fairly immediate basis. A student or a family with one or more students looking to secure tutoring assistance is usually primed and ready to make a decision. For Finish Line most customers call with an immediate need and book an initial meeting at the time of the first phone call. Some customers call back in a short period of time after conferring with a spouse. And there are other calls—such as from school administrators—purely seeking information, and Finish Line uses these to again talk about the value of relationships with customers and the interest they have in giving potential customers "all the time they need." And the same holds true for customers seeking language training in Italian. When most students call, they have already decided to take the course.

Similarly, selling livestock and produce from a farm would certainly lend itself to a fairly immediate sales cycle, and sure enough, First Fruits reports that in the early days, most customers were walk-ins, but now they are regulars who reserve livestock ahead of time. Similarly, eggs are on a regular delivery schedule. Spiritours admits to knowing little about this and suggests that she might do further investigation, but then surmises that the sales cycle is typically weeks — the length of time from when a customer becomes aware of the possible tours, then does the investigation, is treated to Spiritours' sales approach (mail or e-mail info, follow-up phone call, invite to an info session), and then may make a decision either on the spot or within a week or two. Making a decision means sending in a registration form and a deposit. Sofia Violins only reports that they sell through dealers and so are not involved in retail level purchasing decisions, while Ideal reports only that the sales cycle depends on the customer—some about a month, others about 4–6 months. Dealerflow is in the pre-revenue stage of existence and so has no answer for this.

In contrast to these, there are two companies, with very involved sales processes and a fairly long sales cycle. These are Mundell & Associates and Netuitive. Mundell & Associates reports a fairly lengthy sales cycle—perhaps up to year—although they have gotten business on fairly short notice at times if it requires their expertise or some other "need" on the part of the customer that might require haste—dissatisfaction with another consultant perhaps. But they also note again the value of the "customer relationship"—if a customer doesn't meet and talk to them, they are not at all likely to get work. Netuitive reports a fairly long, complicated, technical sales cycle as might be expected with a complex software product that is essentially a customized installation and that might sell for anywhere between 50K and up, with an average selling price of 300K. Customers subject the software to a number of evaluative stages that might last from 1 to four months each and that include a pre-evaluation stage, a technical evaluation stage, a cost justification stage, and a purchasing stage.

Some of the most revealing information about an approach to selling is provided by CHB. Again, this is largely a function of the type of service and the likely clientele. This sort of personal coaching demands an almost constant process of selling—but in this case—developing and nurturing a relationship. But here's what CHB has to say.

> It takes in average 3–6 months to develop a client. It is important to be constantly present through useful communication via email or in person. Networking events are most important. I try to have 5 meetings a week to develop new business (prospecting, referral request, networking, sales meeting etc.). Last week I received a call from a client who was overwhelmed when I coached him a couple of times last year. He told me that he realized the benefits of the few sessions we had and that he was about to resume... I started a new client two weeks ago whom I had met repeatedly at Chamber events over a period of three months.[6]

Given this broad range of variation in selling cycles, we followed up with specific questions about the process of selling, specifically the use of sales people or some type of sales force. Our interest here is learning about how each of the businesses actually approaches customers, pitches the product and closes the sale. Is "selling" a well-developed function in these businesses? Is there a strategy in the approach each business takes to target and connect with

---

6. From Survey 3, February 2009.

potential customers? Do they know what works and what doesn't?

Four of our companies use no sales people or a sales force at all. What that actually means is that the owner of the business tends to whatever selling is done. Beyond that, these four have no sales personnel or sales operations staff for their businesses. Three other of the companies, Sofia Violins, Spiritours, and Mundell & Associates have significantly more expansive sales functions, but also differ significantly from each other. Sofia Violins serves the top end of a very vertical market. Violins and other instruments are distributed through a global network of about thirty exclusive agents. Although Sofia meets these agents at conventions and other meetings, communication is principally by phone and e-mail. The company provides no sales training nor any core sales message for agents or buyers. A Sofia newsletter to the agents offers updates on product and market developments, and periodically features one of the dealers. Spiritours has no designated sales force or even a designated salesperson, but they do train employees about their tour products. When a new tour is introduced, employees are expected to study the programs and brochures and participate in a short training that emphasizes tour highlights. The owner encourages employees to assist in delivering information sessions for customers so they can hear customer questions—and Spiritours' answers. There are also YouTube videos connected through the company website which serves as a "sales force" all on its own. Actual photos and commentary from people in previous tours do a rather effective job of both describing the tours and generating interest and enthusiasm and sales.

Mundell & Associates uses a "part-time" professional salesperson outside the business, a person the owner has known for 15 or 20 years. The arrangement allows for about one day per week of the professional's time to sell for Mundell & Associates and to help coordinate Mundell &

Associate's internal sales and marketing effort. Sometimes company staff persons take on assignments and the part-time professional works with them to keep things moving. The owner sets the "vision" and specific guidelines which the sales professional helps to implement.

> When we advertise, we want to portray a very "honest" image of what we do, as transparent as possible, not to oversell ourselves. If possible, we want to convey part of the 'soul' and 'passion' of what we do, the 'something more....It's important to communicate that Mundell & Associates has a different vision...that we are not just wanting to get business for the sake of getting business, but as part of establishing a relationship with the other person.[7]

To achieve this, the company often focuses first on the relationship and how to make someone's life easier as a result of the service they provide. The hoped for result will be that Mundell & Associates earns business because others appreciate working with them and align with their philosophy, and because, of course, they provide high quality service. As the owner further comments:

> Sometimes we spend efforts not considered "marketing" per se, but that actually result in new work coming in. For us, "sales" is really the result of all of our efforts, even those that don't appear to have "'normal value," but result in unexpected Providence.[8]

The one area of business practice where values and principles might be in significant tension with competitive necessities is in the arena of pricing.

Pricing Practices

It is a challenging task in some ways to provide context and depth to a discussion of pricing practices and competitive

---

7. From Survey 4, April 2009.
8. Ibid.

behavior. Much of the challenge stems from the breadth and complexity of the topic. The study of markets and competitive behavior informs an entire branch of microeconomics, industrial organization, and traveling down that path would soon have us embroiled in theory about perfectly competitive markets, imperfectly competitive markets, monopolies, oligopolies, price taking and game theory. And, all that is just a start. This is not to make light of any aspect of industrial organization, for this is indeed the theory that informs not just the fields of marketing and business strategy, but also government intervention in markets. It is the province then of marketers and strategists, but also of academics, civil servants and antitrust practitioners.[9]

But our purpose lies in a slightly different place. We are less interested in examining EOC practices under the microscope of industrial organization theory, and more interested in trying to uncover and understand the thought process and consideration with which these company owners approach the whole question and issue of pricing. It is not at all clear how a company or a business that "places the person at the center of the enterprise" approaches the question of pricing. What this interest shares with microeconomics is an interest in price as the central question in all of competitive behavior. In fact, it would be difficult to raise any other management question to the same level of importance as price. And further, we would argue that it is one area of business that has the potential to manifest deep and closely the values that might be in play.

Perhaps the best place to begin is with what economists would call "price discrimination." This idea stems from an understanding of perfect competition and means that different consumers have different preferences for any given product or service at any given time, and therefore different

---

9.   Tirole, Jean. 1988. The Theory of Industrial Organization. MIT Press, Cambridge MA. p 3.

consumers have a willingness to pay different prices for the same good. Producers therefore attempt to "discriminate" among consumers; that is, to engage in various practices that are aimed at obtaining the highest possible price from every willing consumer. The presumption is that price-maximizing behavior among producers will always be the norm.[10]

This assumption is fundamental, and strong, and un-yielding, and yet, the notion that someone might pay less for the exact same item or service is so anathema to most of us that price discrimination was made illegal. Given the same circumstances, producers must charge the same amount to consumers. And this leads producers to engage in non-price competition, or to find other ways to create the circumstances that will allow them to discriminate. Thus, when price is expanded to include other factors than just the price at the moment of purchase, we could look at coupons, frequent flyer or shopper clubs. Membership only buying clubs, special offers, loyalty programs, and the like are all ways of providing price differences to different groups of consumers. And the internet is making this easier and easier.

At some level economics can make pricing sound very mechanistic and deterministic. But in reality it is a complex and very calculated decision that has both emotional and philosophical dimensions. The tension between "leaving something on the table" and "always commanding the highest possible price" is a very real tension for which any lasting resolution is elusive. In some markets and industries pushing through a price increase or passing along a price in-crease from suppliers to customers is a challenging, nerve-wracking game—one full of temptation to, for example,

---

10. Besanko, David, Dranove, David, Shanley, Mark, and Schaeffer, Scott. 2003. *Economics of Strategy*, 3e. Wiley, John & Sons, Incorporated. p 262. "the starting point for our analysis is the premise that, all else equal, firms would prefer prices to be closer to their monopoly level than to the levels reached under Bertrand or Cournot competition."

collude. Some contracts are won on the basis of a very infinitesimal difference in price. And there are a number of ways of thinking about price—as total procurement cost, or as the amount of cash that must change hands in a given instant. Financing ability changes the price equation as well, and in some cases actual listed price is less important than financing terms, which in itself constitutes a price.

Moreover, as consumers, we equate price with quality, status, and prestige. All of us feel good when we get a price break or a bargain, and there are all sorts of incentives these days that are part of the pricing equation like the loyalty programs mentioned above. Some of us love to haggle and in some cultures, haggling is a preferred and time-honored means of establishing price. Pricing is a loaded and value-laden proposition.

Since pricing decisions must be and are made, there exists a considerable body of received wisdom, distilled from years (centuries) of practice, that allow us to think about and examine pricing practices in a systematic way. For starters, any given price on any given day to any given consumer for any given product or service will fall somewhere between a price that for the producer, is too high to stimulate demand, or too low to nurture any profit.[11] This leads to two fundamental approaches to pricing. Value-based pricing which is intended to stimulate demand and to set a price in some way equal to the value the consumer perceives. And then cost-based pricing, which is a view toward a price that is sufficiently greater than costs so as to allow profits. Value sets the ceiling and costs set the floor.

Ultimately, the owner must make a decision (even what economist refer to as "price-takers" are making decisions). In every case that decision is value-laden and strategic. Pricing

---

11. Armstrong, Gary and Kotler, Philip. 2008. *Marketing: An Introduction.* 9e. Prentice Hall, Saddle River, NJ., p. 259: "The price the company charges will fall somewhere between one that is too high to produce any demand and one that is too low to produce any profit."

has enormous implications for the business. Sales growth, market share, competitive parity, customer relationships, are all connected in some way to pricing. More philosophically, price is where competitors meet each other. It is, in some way, the point at which an ongoing encounter occurs both with competitors and with consumers. So, do our EOC companies offer any new and noteworthy insight into this whole question? As a way of getting to their philosophical approaches and value drivers, we simply asked them, in a very open-ended way, to describe their pricing decisions. Their responses were a bit sparse—almost as though they don't spend a lot of time or energy with these decisions; almost as though it's not a big deal.

Perhaps not surprisingly our EOC companies overwhelmingly adopt a cost-based approach to pricing. Six of the 10 companies responded very simply and straightforwardly that covering costs was their first and primary consideration. These six would be Netuitive, Mundell & Associates, Finish Line, Spiritours, Arc-en-Saisons, and CHB. Spiritours, of course, offers unique customized travel tours and therefore individually prices each one—and bases the pricing decision on their anticipated costs plus a 15% commission. Netuitive and Mundell & Associates take a somewhat more sophisticated approach. Netuitive uses a published price list that is periodically updated and the 2009 revision actually included price increases that more accurately reflected the extent to which larger customers consumed company resources, which is certainly a cost based approach. The existence of a price list moreover would suggest that their software products are standardized enough to permit a price list. In contrast, Mundell & Associates has no standardized products, and so has no published price list. Each of their jobs is unique and usually, non-repetitive and so each is individually priced. However, they have developed a standardized fee schedule of the billable rates for certain types of services that are used to develop the individual prices. The billable rates include standard multipliers for the recovery of overhead costs and the like. So, again, this is a classic cost-based approach to pricing.

But both of these companies are attentive and cognizant of other factors and influences on price. Netuitive, in addition to costs, also considers the value perception of the customer, and particularly the specific context surrounding each customer at the point in time of a sale. They note that their software products are "add-on" products, which is to say, that customers add their software as an additional program to already existing programs and customers are not willing to concede that the value of any add-on product can exceed the price (or to them, the cost) of the original software. Netuitive maintains that pricing decisions are first a question of costs, then of value, and then of context (the nature of this add-on phenomenon). After consideration of these three criteria, they then consider competitors prices, but they claim they do not react to that, and admit that in many cases their prices are higher than their competitors'. Strategically, Mundell & Associates strives to keep their services at a sufficient level of sophistication that pricing against competitors becomes a non-issue.[12] They do not engage in bidding on competitive low-price winner opportunities, and they pour significant resources into marinating a technological advantage over their competitors. They strive to take on business that no one else can do.

Two additional companies engage in a very strategic approach to pricing decisions, but the strategies are quite different. First Fruits sells agricultural products and they have made a conscious decision to keep prices "low" (presumably this means compared to competition) in order to insure that these perishable food products are almost always sold and the company doesn't have to contend with higher costs from spoilage. They also maintain that the "low" price policy is designed to counteract recent increases in food and

---

12. Preliminary field interviews, June 2007.

fuel prices. Sofia Violins pursues a pricing approach that is focused on positioning. They have a published price list and every instrument carries an unlimited warranty, but they are deliberately seeking to price products at a point below individually crafted and handmade instruments, but above any sort of mass-produced products.[13]

Ideal is the only company that specifically mentions comparison to competitors as the ultimate basis for their pricing decisions. But prior to this competitive comparison, the owners specifically consider both direct costs and fixed costs, and also perceived value to the customer. Five of the companies, Netuitive, Mundell & Associates, Spiritours, CHB and Arc-en-Saisons, four of which we've already noted as using essentially a cost-based approach, do however, compare their pricing to competition, or are aware of how their pricing compares to competitors, and report that the cost based approach has resulted in pricing that is *higher* than competitive prices. In these instances, these four owners are ready to defend their pricing on the basis of value delivered to the customer. This, of course, harkens back to the discussion which opened this chapter, namely, the ability to articulate a unique product or service advantage. Thus, there exists also a clear understanding that while pricing is driven by costs, it is also justified by value.

Arc-en-Saisons presents this understanding quite well. As a provider of commercial maintenance services, landscaping is included in their portfolio of services, and, using the example of tree trimming or hedge trimming, the owner explains that it's possible to simply run a trimmer over the hedge and be done in minutes. But it is also possible to carefully remove dead or dying limbs, and shape the hedge or tree to promote growth and health. The result is a very satisfied customer who may not even be aware of the cause of that satisfaction. This is what Arc-en-Saisons means by value and this is what leads to a particular price;

---

13. Ibid.

the cost required to provide this value. Arc-en-Saisons knows the going market price is for similar services and that their price can sometimes be three times that market level. His explanation to prospective customers when they bring up this question is that the price given is for the work requested and Arc-en-Saisons will guarantee the work and their satisfaction. But by satisfaction, Arc-en-Saisons means *"worry-free."* The owner commits to removing any customer concerns and maintains there is really no market price for that commitment.

Summary Observations

There are two things that emerge strikingly from this discussion about competition and competitive practices. The first is the clarity with which these EOC business owners view what they do as less a business and more a set of relationships, and that this *perspective* provides a competitive advantage. Let us try to elaborate. The existence of a business as a set of relationships would seem at first to be a radical idea. It certainly doesn't receive much scrutiny in the academy or much currency among practitioners. But, upon reflection, it takes on the status of incontrovertible fact. A business certainly is a set of relationships. EOC businesses are no different from any other business in this regard — factually. But, it is the owner's perspective that seems to make the difference. It is as though this perspective allows the owners to make decisions and adopt practices that are uncommon. We might even say this perspective represents a moral choice that in turn fuels competitive advantage.

The second thing is a rather relaxed attitude toward the competitive practices of selling and pricing. Perhaps by necessity, perhaps by choice, these businesses seem to take a passive approach to sales. Some of the smaller businesses clearly do not have the resources to train and support a sales staff, and yet the owners did not designate themselves as the sales force (which, de facto, they are). Spiritours has a fairly sophisticated website and does talk about preparing regular employees to answer customers' questions; but this begs the question of how and why potential customers are attracted to Spiritours in the first place. It's word-of-mouth again. There's not much planning required for word-of-mouth promotion, nor is there much control. And how does one measure progress? Sofia's agents and Mundell & Associates' professional sales person notwithstanding, none of the companies so far has identified or described sales or a sales force as a potent tool for their success. Is goodness alone, or even dependence on Providence, an actual sales strategy?

It is similar with pricing. While there appears to be a combination of real business savvy and real sensitivity to the role that price plays in allowing these companies to serve their customers, it seems simple and straightforward. Covering costs is a major consideration mentioned by Netuitive, Mundell & Associates, First Fruits, Ideal, Tutor's Inc and Spiritours. First Fruits exhibits a fairly sophisticated understanding of the relationship between current pricing and future costs, and customer value- or perceived customer value—is also a major consideration mentioned by Netuitive, First Fruits, Ideal, and Spiritours. Mundell & Associates, Sofia, and Ideal also seem to enjoy some significant advantage relative to competition—real technical expertise, or niche markets. We discussed this at some length in Chapter 3. Arc-en-Saisons adds an interesting perspective. While they clearly understand the power of price, they are adamant about its irrelevance. They know they lose business because of their prices and that they could lower them and still make money, but they appear to take the high ground here. In some circles of luxury goods that would be a deliberate strategy, but it is a bit jarring to find in commercial services. Perhaps the clearest statement of an EOC approach to pricing is to add up the costs, check the competition, and go ahead.

Chapter Four

EOC Companies:
Business
Processes and Work Design

> Reengineering... involves going back to the
> beginning and inventing a better way of doing
> work.[1]

In 1993, Michael Hammer and James Champy published
their landmark book, *Reengineering the Corporation: A
Manifesto for Business Revolution.* Their central argument
was that for well over a century business practices had been
shaped by the demand for efficiency and that work practices
and processes bore this out. In order to make goods and
services widely available to larger and larger numbers of
people, those goods and services needed to be produced at
lower and lower costs. This drove the need for specializa-
tion, for the division of labor, for the assembly line, and
for automation. Hammer and Champy argue that this phenomenon led to business practices that became inflexible,
rigid, and unresponsive to changing customer demands and
to changing technologies. In their view, process reengineering—inventing a better way of doing work—is necessary
to provide companies with modern competitive capabilities.

We begin this chapter with their words not because
we intend to hold up EOC companies as examples of

---

1. Hammer, Michael and Champy, James, 1993. *Reengineering the Corporation: A Manifesto for Business Revolution.* New York, HarperCollins. p 31.

reengineered companies (most of them are fairly new start-ups and the idea of remaking themselves just doesn't apply) but to highlight that work processes, job design, and internal operations are crucial aspects of any company. For Hammer and Champy, business process design is the difference between companies that are viable and sustainable and those that are not.[2] So, too, business processes are important for EOC companies, and we set out to learn what we could about how they manage credit, financing, and investment decisions, how they approach planning, how they think about quality and measuring performance, how they work with suppliers, and how they manage the work environment. As we explored these questions we were mindful that attitudes toward people and the work we ask them to do are embedded in any discussion of business processes. As Robert Greenleaf reminds us, "The work exists for the person as much as the person exists for the work."[3] We therefore also tried to explore the attention paid to people in factors of job design, in the creation of incentives, in the longer term development of people, and in attitudes toward teamwork and employee participation. This chapter includes our finding on all of these questions, beginning with credit and financing, especially during the start-up phase.

Business Process Design

Most of the owners started their EOC businesses as natural extensions of what they were already doing, putting their skills and interests to work for them rather than for an employer. Several owners worked alone from the start and still prefer it that way — "solopreneurs" as one put it. These were not, high-dollar, bet-the-farm kinds of undertakings, but logical next steps that might even be described as income replacement strategies. Startup risks were primarily

---

2. Hammer and Champy, pp 10–11.
3. Greenleaf, Robert. 1977. *Servant Leadership: A Journey in to the Nature of Legitimate Power & Greatness.* New York: Paulist Press. p 154.

opportunity costs, i.e., other employment options or career tracks not pursued at this time. Most relied on personal savings and frugality to bridge the gap between startup and business earnings adequate to replace previous incomes. The owners also seemed to have had modest expectations for growth and wealth accumulation. The exceptions, Dealerflow and Netuitive for example, were dealing with specialized products or product/service packages that required a variety of skills and professional specialties. Creating the businesses and getting into production meant assembling teams from the start; for this they needed significant capital infusions. Others, like Spiritours and Mundell & Associates, assembled those teams and materials too, but they did so as they could afford to over time. Sofia Violins was already an established enterprise the owner chose to make an EOC business.

No special institutional or legal approval is required for a business to operate as an EOC company. There are no rules about how EOC businesses must run. As Luigino Bruni has pointed out, the EOC does not represent an important innovation with regard to "different" or "alternative" forms of business enterprise.[4] EOC companies play by the same rules and in the same environments as their competition. From an operating standpoint, therefore, we would expect them to be dealing with similar operating challenges regarding business processes. We begin by exploring how they approach investment decisions and opportunities.

Financial Investments: Investment in facilities and equipment establishes a baseline for capacity and the costs of ordinary operations in any business, but other generalizations and best practices about such investments really make sense only among businesses producing comparable services or products. However, despite the variety

---

4. Bruni, Luigino. 2002. *The Economy of Communion: Toward a Multi-Dimensional Economic Culture*. New York, New City Press. p 11.

of businesses represented among our companies, when it comes to investing in equipment and facilities the owners *act conservatively*, choosing to *"bootstrap"* operations, to grow slowly and even to stay small rather than take on debt.

It is fair to say that most of these businesses started lean and have stayed lean in regard to investments in equipment and facilities. More complexity and more employees naturally require more investment. But a common theme regarding investments seems to be to *acquire the minimum necessary*; to not overspend or invest beyond what is necessary. Mundell & Associates' investment in geophysical equipment, computers, specialized software, and vehicles is significant today, but it was purchased out of operating funds over a period of years and maintained or replaced on schedule; practices that improve the accuracy of forecasting and estimating capital needs. Mundell rents equipment it uses less frequently, but it also has significant investment in high tech equipment and sets aside funds each year for replacements, upgrades and service contracts. The owner describes himself as a very conservative risk taker, an attitude reflected even today in the way he finances operations:

> I was blessed—during the first 10 years I never had to take out a loan, but did it all on my savings and the receipts of the company. Now I have a $300K line of credit with the bank that I only tap into if I am really desperate. [5]

The owner of Sofia Violins echoes that sentiment, describing himself as conservative. "There has been equipment commercial financing and a revolving bank line of credit; but no loans from family and friends or use of retirement funds." [6]

Netuitive is the only company that depended on outside venture capital at startup. Their product was not fully

---

5. From Survey 7, September 2009.
6. Ibid.

developed or tested and market acceptance was slower than imagined. On this steep learning curve and with no revenue coming in, space, servers, routers, software and other equipment still had to be paid for. You never know, says Netuitive's CEO, what financing needs may be when a "disruptive innovation" *"... gets out of the invention stage and when it reaches commercial stage... You can make analogies with other similar projects, but you only really know once customers start paying..."* It took a few years, but today revenue from operations is adequate to pay for space and equipment. Would he do this again? If he were to start on EOC business on his own, says the CEO, he would be careful to retain majority ownership, *"in order to preserve the culture and the mission of the business versus having to respond to investors and other priorities."*[7]

Most of the owners used personal savings and business revenues to finance space and equipment, but the nature of their businesses made significant investments unnecessary. In fact the low investment was a primary factor for Terra Nuova's owner in turning an artistic craft into a home-based business that required little equipment or space. *"This fit perfectly with my attitudes on risk. My obligation to pay back (a loan) would have weighed heavily."*[8] Even First Fruit's owner was able to avoid any kind of debt at startup, despite the need to buy livestock and some heavy equipment. *"My preference is to fund with personal savings and only go forward with that as far as I can. I have seen people go under in startups..."* Only the owner of CHB reported borrowing money to purchase office equipment. He describes himself as having a *"fairly big tolerance for risk."*[9]

Planning: Whether a company offers eggs, goats, violins, improved academic performance, repaired ceramics,

---

7. Ibid.
8. Ibid.
9. All quotes are from the respective Survey 7, September 2009.

more effective leaders, remediated land, safer work environments, language skills, global travel, or service of computer banking systems—the underlying workflow of the business always has more complexity than meets the eye. What or who should be included in the workflow depends on multiple factors. For the owner of La Parola, for example, the customer initiates the workflow. For Terra Nuova, the process begins when the damaged object arrives. We use the term "work flow" here to refer to the overall processes and individual steps necessary to initiate a task and bring it efficiently to completion, whether that task is making a product, delivering a service, or completing a related function that allows either to happen. Managing costs and, therefore profitability, is all about managing elements specified in the whole production chain, including the supply chain—material and human inputs, speed, output, quality, waste, etc. Specifically, it's about identifying where value is added (or not added), what that value is, whether a step or input may be inefficient, missing, too costly, redundant or unnecessary.[10] So when we asked the companies in this study about workflow, we did not ask for detailed descriptions of how things get done. We asked about the planning methods instead because it is at the planning level, rather than the doing level, that the complexity needs to be managed.

EOC business owners are *planners.* They see the value of planning whether they are individuals planning their own work, or managers planning the work of others. The owners seem to see basic value and need for planning—as a tool for making things happen that *should* happen. But the owners also recognize the interactive and sometimes useful feedback that comes from monitoring the planning process. Nearly every owner acknowledged resource planning and

---

10. Heizer, Jay, and Render, Barry. 2010. *Operations Management.* 10th edition. New Jersey, Prentice Hall, pp. 259–262.

scheduling. Project planning and tracking customer orders were also widely used as were tracking of processing times. While there is variation among their descriptions, the owners also clearly know that planning makes a difference, and in some interesting ways. When a student walks through the doors of La Parola, the owner needs to be able to respond effectively to "all possible levels of knowledge of Italian." Resource planning, she says, makes her ready to use "knowledge of learning processes, grammar and syntax of language and guest language, teaching skills, group dynamic skills and cultural awareness." The owner of Finish Line also regards resource planning as key — "Without resource planning... we're out of business." [11] Mundell's owner describes how reviewing processing times can help him identify coaching needs that, when addressed, strengthens an employee's capabilities and improves performance. Netutive has adopted an "agile development methodology" in R&D intended to increase productivity and alignment with business needs. The process depends on daily review and feedback sessions. Tracking orders and measuring process times also provide data crucial in identifying best practices. In other words, the owners use planning not merely as calendars or allocation tools, but as the source of information to improve performance.

Measuring Quality and Performance. In a similar fashion, EOC business owners are concerned with measuring and managing key quality and performance variables. They want to know how they're doing. Clarity and precision about what they are measuring varies. Methods for gathering and analyzing information vary too. Levels of complexity and specificity vary, as one would expect given the type and size of these businesses. But one way or another they regularly measure budget, quality and process performance.

---

11. From Survey 9, November 2009.

Owners cite an interesting mix of quality goals, including on time, on budget, accurate, client interaction, joy of students, and reaching reciprocity. They vary, too, in how they specifying target goals, measure them, and use the information. Target goals may be specified in numbers or percentages, or in less-defined terms like "consistency," "stability," "client happiness" with a service and "going the extra mile." More often than not the businesses use simple, direct and intuitive approaches in observing quality: "eye-balling," "getting feedback from the client, "taking the pulse of clients" and looking at "the quality of collaboration and teamwork." When measuring quality they like to include customers and employees at all levels. At Mundell & Associates, project teams and "all levels" participate in the processes, and anyone at any level can suggest a modification or even a "new standard." Similar cross-functional approaches that include employees from all levels are used at Netuitive and Finish Line.

Working With Suppliers. The companies recognize, as well, that apart from what they can control, other factors also influence the quality of their products and services — suppliers, for example. They tend to pay close attention to supplier performance and relationships. As the owner of First Fruits succinctly puts it... *the quality of the feed affects the quality of the eggs.* The impact of supplier relationships is obvious to Sofia Violins. The company tries to be very clear in communicating detailed quality specifications for suppliers. *"We do this in a non-threatening (helpful) way. Our attitude, volume of orders and quick-to-pay policy encourage suppliers to pay attention to our needs. It is not unusual to be told that our quality standards have helped them upgrade their products."*[12]

Netuitive relies on external vendors for hardware and software-hardware to provide critical pieces of their end

---

12. Ibid.

solutions, so they seek the same quality of relationships with suppliers as they do with people inside the company. *"We frequently refer to building partnership on a win-win basis where we try to deeply understand each other's requirements before engaging in doing business together,"* [13] says the CEO. And the concern for quality goes both ways. Sometimes the external providers are much larger companies and they require Netuitive to go through technical certification processes to ensure compliance with their own technical quality standards. Obtaining this certification is very important to Netuitive's customers whose concern is to integrate seamlessly Netuitive technology with their larger technical ecosystem. So the relationships go full circle: from supplier to company to customer and back again.

Sometimes it's not easy to distinguish a collaborator's role: is this a supplier or an employee? At Finish Line, for example, the owner raises the question of defining relationships: "If we consider our consultants as suppliers, they are critical to ensuring the quality of services since they provide most of them." Mundell's owner recognizes the key role suppliers play in ensuring the quality of the company's services: "They can make or break a reputation." Mundell wants 100 percent accuracy for lab reports, and to get that they sometimes blindly submit QA/QC samples to judge the accuracy of their work. The important measurements for drilling are percentage uptime on a project and percentage completion on time and on budget. "Unless, they have told us, we expect them to be on time and on budget, the same as our clients do," says the owner.

The Work Environment. Investments in space and equipment and even in intellectual property obviously depend on the nature of the business. Competitive factors and strategic choices make a difference too. In some competitive environments, the operations of a business, an

---

13. Ibid.

ability to respond quickly and gracefully (nimbly) to new products, delivery methods or marketing practices may be critical.[14] So, we were interested in how nimble the EOC businesses might be, or more accurately how important the owners think it is to be able to respond to the unplanned event in the market. Did they regard their business as "fixed and planned" or "fluid and flexible"—and how important was either approach?

While the owners acknowledge the need for planned policies and procedures, or for reasonable consistency in the flow of work in daily operations, they also wanted to be able to move and to change quickly. None described their businesses as fixed and planned. *"Definitely fluid and responsive,"* said the owners of La Parola and Sofia Violins. The other, CHB, struggles with the ongoing challenge of consulting businesses—keeping an even flow of clients: when working with a client there is too little time to do marketing, and when there is time to do marketing there is too little income from clients. Both businesses are, like others in their field, necessarily responding to changes all the time. *"Certainly systems are in place and routinely reviewed and adjusted,"* says the owner of Finish Line. *"And protocols are in place so that daily clerical and administrative work flows smoothly, but for the type of business we are, fluid and responsive is the way to go."* What type of business is that? One where student demand varies seasonally, where demand is likely to peak and decline based on factors the business cannot control, and where customers and needs are constantly changing.

Mundell & Associates, though a consulting business, requires significant investment in space and equipment owing both to its size and the type of big dollar, high tech environmental projects it takes on. Though the company considers itself more fluid and responsive than planned and

---

14. Heizer and Bender, pp. 36–37.

fixed, it has realized the need for balance. Interestingly, the owner recognizes the connection between employee input, access to top management and flexibility. In the owner's own words:

> We just implemented some additional structure to help with administrative things (invoices, etc.). For a small company, we need to be nimble and flexible. Minimize administrative procedures and red tape as much as possible. Everyone at this point has access to the president if they want to offer an idea.[15]

The challenge for Netuitive, the largest of the companies in terms of investment, employment and global reach, is also to balance stability and flexibility, so that clear planning goals focus their attention and resources, while leaving space to be responsive as new elements/conditions arise. How does Netuitive handle this balancing act? Again, in the owner's own words:

> While clear goals/plans help us in the execution of our tasks, we have created some "red flag" mechanisms that allow us to flag issues that require correction either at a task level or in the more general plans. For example, we have a wider staff meeting every Monday that includes not only the executives but also the next layer of management, where we review how we are executing and where "red flags" are raised systematically.
>
> That is one of the main purposes of the staff meeting. We make it a point to tackle them proactively, as we found out that our best ideas and plans came out of small and large crisis. Paradoxically, there is a certain excitement at times that comes out of tackling issues head on and on working on new plans to solve them as we know that these situations of change often make us and our products better. This often results in a revision of plans and a re-setting of our goals.

---

15. From Survey 9, November 2009.

Sometimes, those changes are significant enough to require changes in the yearly goals and for me to have to go to the board to explain why we are making adjustments, etc.[16]

Bottom line, says Netuitive's CEO, the need to have "a clear direction and plan" and the necessity to "adjust" based on new conditions/assumptions is a continual balancing act. "Some employees are more comfortable in rigid plans while others like to be very reactive," says the CEO. "I feel that at Netuitive we strive to achieve the balance mentioned above... we succeed often and sometimes learn from our mistakes."

Processes for People

Looking at the people side of a business takes in a lot of territory. For one group of businesses in our study, people *are* the business; their knowledge and energy channeled directly into a customer service generates revenue. Finish Line, CHB, La Parola and Ideal come to mind here. And in these cases, "operations" require less concern for systems and materials than for meaningful, productive time with customers, where one person is essentially responsible for getting the job done. A second group, though relying heavily on the energy of one person, requires material investments in space and tools to get the job done; here we think of Arc-en-Saisons and First Fruits. For Spiritours the complexity turns to marketing, managing contract employees, customer agreements, and coordinating complex schedules among multiple providers (such as airlines, hotels, and ground transportation). At Mundell & Associates, Sofia Violins and Netuitive the creation and delivery of services or goods is complex enough to require significant investment in space and equipment, and investment in a stable, specialized workforce.

---

16. Ibid.

It's fair to think about the starting point or baseline for growing human capital as the quality of the workforce assembled or hired in the first place. And we will take this up further in the next chapter. In a strictly operational sense, increasing the value of human capital requires continued development and growth, and the cooperation of both managers and workers in planning, taking initiative and creating new experiences. For the EOC, however, there is a goal that transcends even the human capital goal, worthy though it is, and that is to create "communities of loving relationships."[17] For this, says Lorna Gold, who has written extensively on the subject, the EOC draws a picture of what such communities might hold in common, including: investing in the work-force through employee development; using team work and generating team spirit; compensating fairly and appropriately; and encouraging employee participation in decisions. They would also need, says Gold, a "spiritual motive to endure during extreme hardships rather than see the project fail" and a belief in providence.[18]

The questions we address here have more to do with "capital" issues, i.e., what knowledge, abilities and other qualities did the owners need or want to bring into their businesses? We wondered, too, what they might do to strengthen and improve their employees as workers. It was immediately clear to us that the owners viewed their responsibilities as leaders not just to hire and train, but to continue to create opportunities for growth by rewarding and channeling enthusiasm, helping employees work to their strengths, encouraging them to think about career paths, giving them freedom to try new things.

Creating Work and Incentives: None of the companies in our group have gone "all out" in the area of formal job design and only two had worked out formal job descriptions

---

17. Lorna Gold, 2010. *New Financial Horizons: The Emergence of an Economy of Communion.* Hyde Park: New City Press. p 157.
18. Gold, p 158.

for all positions. As one owner who had decided to do without job descriptions said, "It's one of the benefits of being little!" But with or without these elements of traditional operational planning, evidence of concern for employee development in the way they describe positions, define employee requirements and manage the flow of work might be expected.

The owners express a lively interest in their employees; they want competent, hard-working people, but they also want people who will thrive in the company's culture and support its values. Hiring competent employees is clearly a first priority, but attitudes that speak to EOC values are important as well. While only the larger companies in the group had worked out formal job descriptions — in the case of Mundell and Netuitive complete inventories of descriptions — all of the owners readily described the sets of skills, education, experience of credentials necessary for success in particular jobs. They focused on knowing what was necessary to accomplish the work more than on personal attributes or attitudes, though a few indirect references to EOC values did come up. Finish Line' owner, for example, in stressing "people ability" as a key attribute, said they want employees who know "that each person in front of you is a treasure." For La Parola's owner accomplishing her work meant that she "placed the student at the center of all that she did." And Netuitive's CEO stressed that *"adherence to company values is a must."* Those values, promoted openly and consistently within the company, do reflect the EOC but are not unique to EOC. Mundell & Associates explains to prospective employees that the company expects employees to treat co-workers, clients, and suppliers with respect in every aspect of operations, "demonstrating patience, trust and positive regard for the other in every work relationship." Ultimately, the owner said, employees are "the face and the spirit of the business and its EOC values," so it is essential that employees be able to interact authentically with clients in ways that reflect those values.

In those companies with larger employee groups we saw well-conceived approaches to defining and organizing jobs. At Mundell & Associates organizational charts detail reporting and accountability relationships in a well-organized system of roles and responsibilities. And the impetus for this detail came from the employees themselves, especially young employees who expressed a need to see movement toward their goals. Every position at Mundell has a formal description that specifies experience levels, special requirements, and various tasks, e.g., field and administrative activities, sales and marketing, and expectations for professional development project leaders, for consulting principals and senior consultants. Descriptions differentiate positions within levels too, based on factors like field work vs. office work, technical writing vs. quantitative analysis and computer analysis vs. client interaction.

Differentiation helps people to work to their strengths and to do more of what excites them. It was also intended to help them see avenues for movement in the company, how salary relates to these positions and how clients may be expected to be charged based on the employee skill requirements. Mundell's performance review system aligns with job descriptions, with ratings for detailed aspects of technical work, teamwork, and the quality of the employee's work overall. Reviews also address the what the owner calls "non techie" areas—adherence to operational polices in safety, production, and relationships with clients, vendors, contractors, co-workers and supervisors. Creativity, reliability and initiative, and ethical, honest, transparent behavior in all areas of work are also part of annual reviews.

Finish Line emphasizes teaching credentials and experience, but occasionally makes exceptions for individuals with deep knowledge in a discipline *and* philosophies "right in line with the EOC principles." La Parola and Ideal

Safety operate in much the same way, starting with well-prepared and/or credentialed people and turning them loose to do their work. Spiritours values experience in the travel industry, but when it comes down to it "enthusiasm" is the first characteristic the owner seeks, seemingly because it leads to employee growth and the company's good. In the owner's words: *"Enthusiasm and motivation are the first characteristics to look for because the employee (who) is really enthusiastic about his/her work will learn faster, do a better job and create a nicer atmosphere."*[19]

Organizational charts detail reporting and accountability relationships in a well-organized system of roles and responsibilities at Mundell & Associates. Every position has a formal description specifying experience levels, unique requirements, and tasks associated with different types and levels of responsibility; as a set, these descriptions outline a technical and management career path. These were created with on-the-job training in mind and to help get experience in multiple areas: field work and technical work, technical writing, quantitative analysis, computer analysis and client interaction. What is the impetus for such attention and detail? Young employees expressed a need to see movement toward their goals and to understand better their contributions to the company. Besides providing a "road map" for employee development, the owner sees three other advantages to this careful approach: first, it relates pay to positions; second, it helps employees understand how skill levels required in particular projects influence what the client is charged; and third, it invites people to work to their strengths and to do more of what excites them. Besides creating a career "road map," Mundell offers a broad set of development options that apply directly to employees' ongoing work. Among these are exposing them to a variety of projects, from basics to the more challenging "career builders"; training

---

19. From Survey 2, September 2008.

on numerous subjects, including standard methods, field techniques and technology; seminars, courses and work on advanced degrees (tuition reimbursed); dues paid to at least one professional organization per year; incentives for gaining professional registration, e.g., as a professional engineer or geologist; and other special presentations.

Netuitive's job descriptions for managers typically contain more detail than those for technical and entry level positions. But all descriptions include four categories of requirements: professional qualifications, education, experience and cultural fit. Professional staff must have formal training and expertise in specific domains (e.g., software development skills for developers and Ph.D. in math or computer science for research roles). The company expects employees to be able to interact effectively with customers, who tend to be people with a sophisticated understanding of business and technology. Technical and professional staff are college graduates at a minimum; the company helps finance college coursework for administrative staff who come in with a bachelor's degree.

In addition to internal promotions and some lateral role exchanges, Netuitive encourages employee development by incorporating personal development plans in annual reviews; bringing in skilled trainers for company meetings; encouraging participation in professional organizations; and encouraging advanced certification or progress toward developing industry/domain expertise. Perhaps most important, says the CEO, *"We know that a key to keeping our best employees motivated is to continuously 'stretch' them in new directions and allow them to develop the best they can."* Some of their best managers, says the CEO, have been developed and promoted within the business. Though turnover has been low, sometimes things do not go as planned, as the CEO explains:

The few times we have lost employees was not because they didn't like the company or were not well-treated or compensated...it's that we could not provide a way for them to achieve their professional dreams...even if we tried hard. Sometimes we need to recognize we can't offer a certain opportunity. Then we make it a point to help the employee find his next best job...and they end up becoming great references for our company.[20]

The owner of Sofia Violins describes his company as "unusually unstructured" and having "extremely responsible long term employees who are given a lot of freedom." Quality is *the* key asset for Sofia Violins' violins, a reputation created by the skills of the company's violinmakers. The owner describes them as, *"the most important asset in our business"* and as *"highly motivated to make instruments we can be proud of."* The owner has no desire to "micromanage," preferring, he says, "employees who do not need to be 'supervised.'" He takes pride in giving *"employees unusual freedom to manage themselves and their job."* But he also takes development efforts seriously, paying for outside training, and also focusing on involvement and encouragement. *"We are very instrumental in helping each person develop their skills and personal reputation as a master violinmaker. For example, we use our resources to help our makers sell 'personal' instruments they make outside of company time....we are not involved in profiting..."*[21]

Long Term Development: Building and refining employee skills does more than create a stronger, more stable workforce. It also supports collaborative thinking, culture and values over the long run. Any company with younger, more professional employees faces the challenge of longer term retention. When we asked the owners about their longer term strategies, most had little to report, though one

20. From Survey 9, November 2009.
21. Ibid.

described the long term focus as too "intangible." But from those who had given some thought to this question, we heard some interesting ideas.

In some ways, Mundell & Associates' owner views employee development plans as an answer to employee retention and growth. Paying for advanced degrees, encouraging professional engagement, and creating a career path with increasingly more challenging jobs—such practices help employees form a vision for their future with the company. Though it is not on the table yet, Mundell & Associates' owner thinks that employee ownership, at least among senior employees, may be the way for the company to continue when the time comes for him to leave.

At Netuitive every employee is a stock holder, so every employee has real financial ties to the long term success of the business. The CEO sees employee stock ownership is a strategy for ensuring alignment and recognition of employee contributions to the company. Still, he says, separate from stock ownership is a more important benefit and long term incentive: the opportunity to experience a highly collaborative and open environment in which results equal or exceed those of hierarchical businesses driven by a numbers-only mentality. In the CEO's words: *"We feel that we help our employees become better professionals and better human beings at the same time. That is at the end probably our biggest reward for us and for them."*[22]

Sofia's owner believes that one of the industry giants will want to acquire his company someday, but would a new owner would keep the current employees? That he does not know and it bothers him. In the long run, he says, employees' personal skills and reputations are their best insurance to continue pleasant and fruitful careers as luthiers. So he tries to promote his employees' skills and reputations separate from the company. The intent, he says, is to give

---

22. Ibid.

them the option to become private violin makers who can make good livings working on their own with commissions to make instruments for professional players. He believes the employees understand clearly what he is doing and why, and they seem deeply grateful.

Teamwork: In describing business practices, the owners' talk is full of "we," and "us," "working together" and "teams" and references to collaborative, open environments. Even the owner of Arc-en-Saisons, who has no fulltime employees, talks in first person plural—because he automatically includes his wife and most trusted advisor, in company problems and decisions. Spiritours' owner assiduously avoids hierarchical language, especially with her close reports. "We are a team," she says. The very nature of Mundell's business dictates the use of teams—permanent, temporary, functional, cross-functional, you name it. And the owner tries to use these teams for more than mere oversight or task functions. They have become opportunities for mentoring, teaching, and working on leadership skills, for motivating and rewarding people, for performance assessment and for fun. Sofia Violins also relies on team work, but the approach here is to think of the organization as one big team by including everyone in planning and decision making.

Participation: At Spiritours and Finish Line, employee "participation" in decision-making seems simply to be a way of life. Says Finish Line' owner, *"Business decisions are made on a consensus basis—we are all involved."* Mundell's owner described a more "as needed," or consultative version. *"We solicit input from all levels, even the youngest, who can see 'new market' possibilities. We solicit input on key decisions, and see what everyone says... Many have seen their ideas implemented, and everyone knows it was their idea."* Sofia Violins describes its practices in terms that suggest both consultative input and full participation in decision-making, but something more: *"All of our*

people within the organization are involved in planning
and decision making. We are like a Japanese company in
soliciting everyone's input." And from Netuitive comes a
description that captures both the varieties of participation
and the system-wide value of participative techniques, particularly in individual development, supporting teamwork
and information sharing:

> We involve employees quite extensively in business plan-
> ning and decision-making. This happens for ad hoc projects
> as well as for our most important yearly/quarterly goal set-
> tings. We often create ad-hoc project teams to come up with
> a plan. The members of the team often cross departmental
> and hierarchical boundaries. We pay particular importance
> to the employees that are on the front lines (vs. managing
> in the office) as they are closest to our customers and in the
> best position to listen and understand their needs. ...we oper-
> ate in an environment of shared goals, empowerment, strong
> alignment (from top to bottom in the company) and of joint
> responsibility.[23]

In some ways teamwork and employee participation
are variations on a theme: that knowledge and power do
not lie in the mind(s) of top management alone. From an
operational perspective and a competitive one, teamwork
and participative decision-making are being used in these
companies both to contribute to human development and to
enhance efficiency and effectiveness. In very basic ways,
teamwork and participation operationalize EOC values for
relationships, community, and seeing the individual person.
From the owners we heard evidence that together teamwork
and participation serve to increase knowledge, share information, stay in touch with the customer, get feedback from
the front lines, align objectives, encourage transparency,

---

23. Ibid.

share goals, power and ownership, and solve who knows how many problems.

Summary Observations

In the fundaments of operations these EOC companies look very much like other businesses. They plan, they measure and they demonstrate concern for efficiency and for quality. They understand the importance of pleasing their customers and the significance of having good sup- plies — and good relationships with suppliers. Most of them started with modest financing and remained conservative in terms of debt and capital investment. Their organic growth, often a bootstrap approach, has allowed them to grow and invest in their businesses without assuming undue risk or experiencing radical shifts in processes or people. What we see here is good, solid operational management and a con- cern for process effectiveness and efficiency. We see little evidence of a uniquely EOC approach in operations. More importantly, perhaps, we see nothing that is out of harmony with it either.

On the human side of operations, however, we see more evidence of the EOC ideals and an imprint of EOC thinking in regard to putting the person at the center of the enterprise, creating and sustaining relationships, teamwork, participa- tion, and employee development. Good work design, posi- tive human interaction, opportunities for learning, empha- sizing the person more than the work itself — practices such as these are typical concerns for the EOC companies in this study. Leaders express a strong sense of duty for creating work environments where people can do and be their best, where they can grow personally and where mutual trust and support among co-workers encourages the growth and the potential of all. Increasing the human capital resource is regarded as a shared responsibility and treated as a priority, not merely a managerial function. Comments from EOC leaders in this study also indicate a sensitive and nuanced understanding of what employee well-being means, both now and in the long term. Evidence of this understanding lies, in fact, in the many and various ways they attempt to inspire excellent performance, including both extrinsic incentives and attention to the intrinsic rewards of work. Emphasis on collaborative decision-making and sharing credit for success are but some of the everyday practices indicative of a leadership perspective that assumes employees share their own hopes for fulfillment and desire to do something good. Growing employee knowledge, capability, flexibility and dedication — or effectively managing human capital — are understood to benefit the business, not just as an economic entity, but as a community of work.

Chapter Five

EOC Companies:
Employees and Hiring Practices

> The executives who ignited the transforma-
> tions from good to great did not first figure out
> where to drive the bus and then get people to
> take it there. No, they first got the right peo-
> ple on the bus... and then figured out where to
> drive it.[1]

The bus, and the idea of getting people on the bus,
is the metaphor for companies, and their recruiting
and hiring practices, used by Jim Collins in his acclaimed
study of great companies. One of the distinguishing and
counter-intuitive characteristics of "great" companies is not
only that they systematically and rigorously look to hire the
right people for the company, but that this was more important than vision, strategy, and management processes. It
doesn't replace vision, strategy, and management processes,
but having the right people goes a long way toward making a company adaptable and flexible and toward providing
intrinsic incentives and motivation. The right people who
can help shape and define the right strategy might propel a
company to greatness. The right strategy without the right
people will not. As Collins succinctly points out; "first
who... then what,"[2] But greatness is not solely a matter of

---

1. Collins, Jim. 2001. *Good to Great*. New York: HarperCollins. p 41.
2. Collins, p 63.

hiring the right people. It requires that those people find their most productive and useful places in the company (what Collins refers to as being in the right seats on the bus), and in then working to keep those people invested and engaged. It requires being what Robert Greenleaf would describe as "people-building institutions."[3] For Greenleaf, people-building is a natural result of servant leadership; and though it may not be the *purpose* of a business, people-building is a distinguishing characteristic of excellence.

All of this strongly suggests that hiring practices might be among the most crucial for any company. But hiring decisions are fraught with complexities. Companies are looking for certain sets of knowledge, experience, skill and, presumably, someone who is a "good fit" for the organization. Hiring can be a very important and crucial activity in a company, particularly a small company, and there is no perfect way to assess the outcome prior to a hiring decision. Despite probationary periods, orientations and mentoring programs, there are failures. The risk is high. In the United States, for example, it is illegal to ask certain questions of applicants and concerns for fairness and equity require that all applicants have an equal opportunity and affirmative action may require careful attention to everything from the wording of ads, to the pool of applicants to actual hiring decisions. Even in right-to-work situations, termination and lay-offs can be very problematic and not just for legal reasons, but because people are involved. At the same time, particularly in the early stages of a company's life, a single hire may be a force that initiates "responsive and adaptive"[4] leadership action, as Selznick describes it, with lasting impact on the shape and values of the organization.

---

3. Greenleaf, Robert K., 1977. *Servant Leadership: A Journey into the Nature of Legitimate Power & Greatness.* New York: Paulist Press. p 53.
4. Selznick, Philip. 1957. *Leadership in Administration.* New York: Harper & Row. p 16.

Hiring practices might be both more crucial and more problematic for EOC companies. For these companies, hiring practices are not only fraught with all of the complexities noted above but also with questions and complexities stemming from participation in the EOC and its grounding in faith. Moreover, the EOC begins with a distinctive commitment to a community intended to influence a company's decisions and actions, which, according to the "institutionalizing" view of organizations, will influence what a company becomes. Success in building community may be as important as profitability, size and growth in orienting the decisions of an EOC company. In Chiara Lubich's view, community goes to the very purpose of an EOC business. These businesses propose something different, she would propose. For them, the true meaning of all their economic activities lies not in the economic transaction *per se*, but in making it a 'meeting place' in the deepest sense of the word: a place of communion.[5] For EOC companies, "getting the right people on the bus" means considering faith and commitment to shared ideals in the hiring process. It also means thinking past "greatness" or "excellence" to "community." We sought then to understand how EOC companies navigated these complex waters and asked them not only about their hiring practices, but also their approaches to orientation of new employees and to the long term development of the people associated with their companies.

Hiring as a Strategic Activity

Before we turn to specific findings from our companies, let's expand on the importance of hiring and its role moving a company forward. Once considered a support function, the human resource activity of today's corporation is likely to be treated as a key strategic factor, not merely a function,

---

5. Lubich, Chiara. 2006. *Essential Writings*, edited by Michel Vandeleene. Hyde Park: New City Press. p 276.

on a par with line operations, and a key aspect of strategic planning. A strategic HR focus means taking long-term view of HR choices, environmental forces, and a company's "game plan for action."[6] It goes beyond organizing, staffing and compensation, taking an HR voice into problems and problem-solving wherever they occur in the organization. These efforts, it is hoped, will improve performance around the cost, size and distribution of a workforce and enhance workforce planning in light of strategic opportunities and goals. As evidence mounts that organizational effectiveness is influenced by employee selection, training and retention, matters once considered tactical "personnel" issues take on strategic proportions. In larger businesses HR departments may include specialists in compensation and benefits, recruitment, training and a half dozen other areas, and instead of working out of headquarters, staff may be distributed or "embedded" in production and service sites to be closer to the action.

In hiring and training best practices make use of job analysis to develop critical skill sets which can then be integrated into position descriptions, ads, employment interviews, testing and observation. To generate good candidate pools HR savvy companies work on getting ad copy and placement just right, targeting appeals to specific groups and highlighting the company's reputation and promoting practices and values that are likely to attract their target group. It may be commitment to work-life balance or competitive benefits, flexible schedules or even corporate social responsibility. Some employers enlist current employees in recruiting efforts at job fairs. Internet, professional networking and social media supplement or even replace traditional want ads. The best hiring processes start with automated search and screening processes. Using team interviews

---

6. Anthony, William P., Kacmar, K. Michele, and Perrewé, Pamela L. 2010. *Human Resource Management: A Strategic Approach.Boston: City?*Cengage Learning. p 9.

and questions that seek specific examples of the applicant's skills, assessing motivation and "fit" with corporate values and putting applicants through relevant task simulations are also among those practices which lead to best hiring outcomes. In general, competitive and legal issues have given rise to a more disciplined "evidence-based" style in human resource management and generated much field research on best practices like those described here.[7]

In smaller businesses and entrepreneurial enterprises, a "personnel" model is likely to prevail—in the person of the owner, entrepreneur or general manager, for whom human resource management is just one of many responsibilities. Some standard corporate practices in hiring may be viewed as beyond their need or beyond their reach. Managers, often already be chronically short on time, may be tempted to take short cuts in hiring. Ironically, the consequences of hiring may be far greater for these smaller companies than for large ones. As one of our HR colleagues put it, "In a small business one poor hiring decision can blow things apart."

Good hiring experiences in small companies look like a scaled down version of good practice in larger companies. They begin with planning, developing well-researched and future-oriented job descriptions before hiring begins, a time-consuming process that the manager may be tempted to skip. But well-crafted job descriptions can be the basis for identifying key requirements—in knowledge, skills and attitudes and experience for particular jobs. Greater clarity about responsibilities, tasks, possible job titles and compensation are likely to happen too and the up-front work aids in preparing recruiting messages that highlight responsibilities, features and practices that make the workplace attractive (e.g., the type of culture, flexible hours, working from home, etc.) and characteristics of outstanding candidates.

---

7. Development Dimensions International and Electronic Recruiting Exchange as quoted in "The Four Hiring Practices of Successful Organizations," Jan. 16, 2002. Source: http://www.inc.com/articles/2002/01/23815.html. Retrieved December, 2013.

Planned and structured team interviews improve chances for hiring success and work best when followed up with adequate post-interview review of candidates. Testing, observing task performance, and inviting applicants back for second or third interviews and checking references thoroughly — every time — also add to chances for success.

However refined and thorough the process may be, hiring is also a very personal matter. A company is a making a decision not just about acquiring talent or expertise, but about a person. Decisions can have far reaching effects — influencing the organization *and* the person hired. Moreover, a hiring decision almost always involves saying "yes" to one person, and "no" to others. The "no" can be difficult, too, both for the company and the candidate. Even saying "yes" has its challenges. Inviting a person into a business means taking a risk and it may mean significantly changing a work group or balancing of talents or interests. Sometimes painful and unanticipated adjustments must be made. Recognizing the complexity of hiring, we decided to ask the owners first to describe their three most recent experiences, with the hope of bypassing the details and going right to the gestalt or story of each. It turned out to be a question most of them did not answer. We highlight here tales from two companies that did:

> Spiritours' owner shared three anecdotes. In the first case, the owner was hiring to replace her assistant, Yvette, and advertised in a virtual magazine with an ad that listed the ideal candidate's professional qualifications, but included "sincere interest in self-development, spirituality, religions and pilgrimages." Screening reduced the pool of applicants to four and the owner enlisted Yvette's help with interviewing and setting up task exercises for the candidates. Afterwards the two independently completed evaluation sheets, compared their impressions and made a decision. Estelle, the new hire, had impressed them both with her enthusiasm and interpersonal skills as well as her professional capabilities. A second

story is like the first, except in this case the final choice was not clear, prompting the owner to "pray to the Holy Spirit for discernment," which led her to decide on her own to hire Charles, who came with ten years in the travel business. The third story was something different. A woman named Aline had heard about Spiritours, liked what she heard, and just walked into the office one day asking for a job. The owner explained that Spiritours was not hiring. Aline persisted, offering to work without pay. This time the owner said it was impossible, even if she wanted to hire Aline, because there was too little space for another employee. That ended the matter—temporarily. After moving to a larger space, the owner reconsidered. She contacted Aline, who joined Spiritours as an unpaid intern. Later, impressed by Aline's skills and the quality of her work, the owner brought her on as a paid employee.

Dealerflow also offered three, each featuring an opportunistic element. The owner explained that all three were truly exceptions to the hiring process in place in the company. In the first story the owner spontaneously offered a job to Mason, an acquaintance of ten years, when he learned quite by chance that Mason was between jobs. In a second situation, reluctantly—and strictly as a courtesy to a friend—Dealerflow's owner was introduced to Ron. Ambivalent at the start, the owner nevertheless listened and found himself interested in what Ron had to say. The more he heard the more the owner began to think that Ron's skills and experiences would be good for Dealerflow, but he was not sure how Ron might fit with the rest of the team. So he offered Ron a short term contract with specific performance goals, to see how he would perform. By the end of the contract Ron had "become part of the fabric" of the Dealerflow team and stayed on as fulltime employee. In the third story, the owner recalled how he had just begun thinking that Dealerflow needed a sales manager when he got a promising lead from a professional network. After several attempts a meeting with Kevin was arranged.

Three interviews and several reference calls later, the owner offered Kevin a job. References and some of the owners' own acquaintances had offered "awesome" feedback. The owner also learned that Kevin had several other offers—for more money, but he came to Dealerflow because he liked idea of working in a tech startup.

In describing these hiring experiences, both the owners gave accounts of fairly well-structured hiring processes in their companies. But in only one of their stories was process the star. The others focus on serendipity, unsolicited offers, prayerful discernment, and creative "trials"—none of which is necessarily opposed to a well-planned process, but they do stretch it. In Spiritours' case there is the juxtaposition of using a very well-planned process for the first hire and going entirely outside the process for the third: job descriptions, ads, screening, interviews and collaborative decision-making on the one hand vs. making room for a walk-in "volunteer" on the other. In Dealerflow's three stories friendship and opportunity seem to trump planning. The owner circumvents but does not entirely ignore the process, proceeding eventually with interviews, reference checks and a contract trial period before making an offer. Spiritours' hiring of Estelle and Yvette come closest to reflecting best HR practice. Whatever the stories reveal about process, however, they also reveal the owners' desire to make decisions for the company; Each reflects a concern for a "good fit" between the new hire and the business, and each, apparently ended up in a successful hire for the respective companies. It also seems clear that owners' concerns went beyond "skill sets." They wanted people who "fit" the company.

Knowledge, Skills and Personal Qualities

As a participant in the EOC, a business sets out to create a culture that makes work a "meeting place in the deepest sense of the word: a communion." Our interest in the hiring practices of the EOC businesses was not primarily with the details and demands of particular jobs. We were more interested in those factors that owners considered most important in hiring for a good "fit" between the employee and the company's culture. But we were also interested in a company's clarity about the knowledge, skills and attitudes necessary to do its basic work—whether that work is tutoring, leading pilgrimage tours, selling goats, or engineering. Thus, in asking about the qualities and characteristics the owners consider most important in the people they hire and why those factors are important, we were really asking about the business and the culture and the human energy that allow both the company and the culture to flourish.

Naturally, the knowledge and skills that our owners highlighted as important to their businesses differed according to type of business. Owners readily put key knowledge and skills into a "strategic" context, explaining their importance in serving the purpose or mission of the business. Some of the attitudes and personal qualities they described as essential for the business seemed to have even more strategic importance than particular skills. Here Mundell & Associates comes to mind. For the owner, it was important to hire employees with a "passion" for the earth projects and for wanting to "do good things for the planet." This kind of passion, the owner says, makes Mundell unique. Finish Line's owner links teaching skills and interpersonal skills to the very heart of the business's reputation, which is, in the owner's words, "all we have."

Whatever else EOC business owners are doing when they hire, they are not focusing exclusively on friends of the EOC or followers of Focolare or Christians, or even people of faith. Given that Spiritours' business is leading tours designed for spiritual and faith-building experiences, it is hardly remarkable that the owner should want employees who understand the project. More interesting, however, is that Spiritours' owner was the only one who identified faith, religion or spirituality in the context of hiring. The owner of Arc-en-Saisons, it must be said, told the story of how, at startup, he believed that an EOC company must be managed by a "new" man. His first hire was, in fact, a young participant in the Focolare—presumably a "new" man. But it turned out that he had a poor work ethic and was undependable as well. Managing that first employee, the owner said, was a challenge that felt "like Jesus forsaken."[8] Subsequently he dropped any mention of EOC or Focolare in hiring, focusing instead on timeliness and steady, dependable work.

Some types of work and essential skills are easier to describe than others. Take Sofia Violins, for instance. All the employees at Sofia, except the owner, are luthiers: they make violins, violas and cellos. The basic elements and skills of their craft have not changed much in centuries. Like luthiers before them, Sofia's craftsmen perform their tasks by the skill of their hands and their understanding of tools, materials, aesthetics and sound. Luthiers in Europe hand-carve and assemble instruments from select, aged acoustic wood grown only in European forests and associated with high quality string instruments. These partially complete instruments are then shipped to Sofia's Indianapolis studio where luthiers enhance and finish them, using special varnishes, pigments, and application techniques to enhance each instrument's beauty and sound.[9] Sofia's owner knows the craft requires eye-to-hand coordination, a love of woodworking, and desire to make instruments to be proud of. Beyond that, however, defining skills and knowledge gets more difficult. Like the best studios of its kind, Sofia's luthiers progress through levels of expertise in their work, with the most experienced developing into "masters." Native talent, training,

---

8. From Field Study Interviews, June 2010.
9. From the company website accessed in May 2011.

and years of supervised effort shape a luthier. These are not the kind of jobs one fills through help-wanted-ads and not the kind of work that lends itself to the language of position descriptions designed to attract large pools of applicants. In fact, says Sofia's owner, luthiers contact Sofia in search of jobs; Sofia does not have to go in search of them. Perhaps because the work is both art and craft, specifying the luthier's essential skills and knowledge is difficult. Managing luthiers requires giving them freedom to manage themselves, says the owner, and therefore he sees nothing to be gained from trying to micromanage them, writing job descriptions, or even writing an employee manual.

The owner of First Fruits also likes people who can work with minimal supervision. Her employees, all part-time workers, are hired because they can do the physical work associated with agriculture and animal husbandry, but also because of their ability to work with little direct supervision. First Fruits' lead associate is typically a college student, and must be licensed for property maintenance as well as have basic skills in carpentry, mechanics, agriculture, and live-stock management. Other qualities of character and attitude are equally important to the lead associate's supervisory role. Recruiting other students to work and overseeing their labor is part of the job and for this reason the owner believes four qualities are essential for someone in this position: reliability, promptness, willingness to take responsibility, and ability to work with minimal supervision.

Since Ideal's owner relies on contract relationships with people who have specific skills related to the safety, health and environmental work, she prefers to hire people with whom she has already "established relationships." Key to these positive and enduring relationships are "trust, being ethical, values and responsibility." These qualities are essential, says Ideal's owner, for building lasting, trusting relationships with clients and associates, which in turn allows Ideal to be both flexible and responsive.

"All Finish Line really has is its reputation and we guard this emphatically," says Finish Line' owner.[10] The owner thus links key employee characteristics to quality and identity. In her business, teaching competence and interpersonal skills are essential, she says. These qualities are so important that when Finish Line interviews a person who is a "maybe" on either characteristic, they prefer to keep looking. Dealerflow takes a similar approach. The right technical skills are essential (e.g., software development, operation), but a possible employee must also "fit the culture." Dealerflow's owner looks for communicative behaviors, respect for others and a desire to collaborate.

Spiritours' owner believes that the employee who is enthusiastic about work will learn faster, do better work and contribute more to the office atmosphere. An even temper, good judgment and sincerity all matter in a prospective employee. But the key personal characteristic necessary for Spiritours employees is a "sincere interest for self-development, spirituality, religions and pilgrimages," qualities that clearly reflect Spiritours' very purpose as a business. Though the company employs a small office staff, it also contracts with experienced tour escorts from among a group of regular associates. Hiring for this group depends more on education, professional skills and experience, with an emphasis on guides who are trained in psychology, philosophy, theology or spiritual coaching, or people who have "developed workshops related to the sites explored during the journeys."[11]

Technical expertise—including skills in software design and development, mathematics, and information systems—are key qualities for Netuitive's technical staff. In addition to education and training in these areas, the company values hands-on experience and a proven track

---

10. From interviews.
11. From the company website accessed in May 2011.

record. But, says the CEO, Netuitive also wants "coachable" employees who are open to new ideas and people, who appreciate teams and work well in them, and whose values "fit the general Netuitive culture." Mundell & Associates shares a similar dual interest in technical qualifications and experience. In both businesses the challenge of completing complex projects requires demonstrable staff expertise.

Having employees with appropriate technical credentials is also essential to sustain Mundell's positioning as a "high quality" provider. Academic credentials from the right schools can be one indication of necessary achievement, though years of experience sometimes substitute. Project management, project experience, the ability to meet deadlines, to solve problems under pressure and to work effectively with clients — all are qualities Mundell seeks in its scientific and engineering staff. In their consulting environment, virtually all employees need to be people-oriented, work well in teams and willingly share their expertise with colleagues and clients. As consultants, says the owner, "Reports are what we produce, not widgets." This makes oral and written communication skills important too. Finally, but not least important, is what the owner calls "passion." He wants to hire people with a *passion* for the environment, for engineering, for science, for problem solving and for the planet. This is something people need to have coming in to the business, he says. "You can train and teach certain technical things, but you can't give someone passion."[12]

As we reflect on our owners' accounts of hiring criteria for new employees we are reminded of how great is the gap between hiring practices in a large corporation and those of a small business, and what a difference it makes to have a specialized HR staff with the money and skills needed to recruit, hire and compensate competitively. When it comes to detailed plans, recruiting, screening, testing, and so on,

---

12. From interviews.

large businesses have all the advantages. But we are not so sure this applies to identifying essential knowledge, skills and attitudes for new hires. And we doubt whether they have any advantage at all over the smaller businesses in this study in identifying the values and personal qualities needed in a particular community of work. In a large business, a new employee may represent only a marginal change in a large workforce. But in small businesses, like the EOC businesses, our owners understand that one person can make a significant difference. We think this understanding is demonstrated in their references to trust, respect, sincerity, independence, enthusiasm and passion as qualities central to the success of the businesses. It also explains their concern for interpersonal skills, relationships, humility, harmony, collaboration, the Golden Rule, teamwork, DNA, mismatch and "fit." But the owners are not hiring just for personality, character or attitudes alone. They are looking as well for necessary and fairly well-defined essential knowledge and skill sets.

What is notably missing among in the owners' accounts of desirable or even helpful characteristics for potential employees is any acquaintance with Focolare or the Economy of Communion. Nor does it appear that religious affiliation or an expressed interest in things spiritual or religious play a role in hiring. One minor exception is Spiritours, which looks for tour guides with a "sincere interest for self-development, spirituality, religions and pilgrimages," language that is, after all, fairly generic. One other exception bears mentioning: While First Fruits' owner suggests no "requirement" in terms of EOC, Focolare, or faith, she does say that all her workers know that she has a "business philosophy based on Christ." With these possible exceptions, and with a concern for "fit," expressed by some of the companies, it is hard to see anything in the hiring criteria that identify these companies as EOC businesses. We suspect this is no oversight.

The Hiring Process

Having a standard approach to hiring and following that approach are two different things. In our group of EOC companies, eight described what might be called their customary approach to hiring. The approaches fall into one of three categories: informal; formal but flexible; and formal and consistent.

We'll place Sofia in the "informal" category, but in some ways it stands on its own. Prospective luthiers seek out Sofia, says the owner, not the other way around.[13] Even the executive VP came in on his own. As an art professor at a nearby university, he stopped in one day to visit a student who was sanding violins at Sofia and just "never left." Another man came to Sofia through a referral from the local Catholic Charities office that was helping to settle Bosnian refugees. He spoke little English, but he had the skill for extensive handwork. Sofia's owner hired him and today he is one of the company's "most committed and flexible employees." Also in the "informal" category are Ideal and First Fruits. Ideal's owner participates in networking events connecting her with professionals who might be available as contract associates should the need arise. She also welcomes referrals from friends and current associates. With strong recommendations or prior acquaintance one interview may be enough to help her decide about an associate. Hiring people who have worked in government saves her doing extensive reference checks because the government will already have done that. In the end, Ideal's owner, says, she learned to trust her "gut feeling." Both Sofia and Ideal are tuned into the importance of hiring and both have processes that have helped them identify effective workers and associates. They rely on the value of credentials and/or demonstrated expertise, personal association and referrals.

---

13. From Survey 2, December 2008.

First Fruits owner basically turns recruiting and hiring over to a "lead associate," who also trains and supervises them.

Dealerflow and Finish Line fall into a "formal but flexible" category. They have standard hiring practices in place, but deviate when necessary. They tend to "recruit" through networks and referrals from trusted sources. Dealerflow's interviews seem to focus on whether a candidate is really able to do what he or she claims. Finish Line owner uses the interview to assess actual teaching knowledge and performance and to look for a normative attitude that fits the Golden Rule. Though Dealerflow has a structured hiring process, the owner occasionally by-passes parts of it for the sake of opportunistic hiring. For example, in two of the unplanned hiring exceptions he bypassed advertising, a pool of candidates and structured interviews, but still used a "rigorous interview" before making an offer. In another case, he created a short-term contract arrangement to observe the behavior, performance capability and "fit" of a prospective employee before bringing him on board full-time. Most of Finish Line' consulting hires are full-time teachers who come referred by other consultants or teachers. Like Ideal, Finish Line has eliminated the need for credential and background checks by hiring from a group where she knows the work has already been done. The hiring interview still holds weight with Finish Line where the emphasis is on trying to see evidence of competence in the field and a disposition "to treat each person as they would like to be treated."

Spiritours, Mundell & Associates and Netuitive all operate in the category we call "formal and consistent." In several ways their processes would compare favorably with best practices in larger corporations. They demonstrate thoughtful position planning linked to strategic business needs before opening a position. They tend to be systematic about how they design positions, and link the wording of the job design to ads or guidelines for recruiters, to screening processes and to questionnaires and interviews. All three companies rely on interview teams, structured interviews and broad participation in the process. By the time candidates come in for interviews, the interview teams will have gone through their materials thoroughly, started background checking and prepared questions to probe for understanding the candidates' abilities, experience and attitudes. None of these companies is shy about stating preferences about personal qualities and values, work attitudes and corporate and cultural philosophies.

Spiritours identifies criteria for hiring, advertises in the places where the ads will count most, emphasizes both technical criteria and personal interest in ads and interviews and also describes the company's internal culture and preferred style of work. The owner personally reviews application letters and resumes and screens them. She and at least one other colleague interview a handful of candidates using structured formats for the process. She then screens further via standardized telephone interviews. Once the field is narrowed, the interview team gets involved. Independently each person in the interview team evaluates candidates, and in a final participative decision process the team shares impressions of candidates and makes a decision. To gauge qualities that resonate with Spiritours values and mission, the job interview probes a candidate's understanding of Spiritours philosophy, which is described along with the EOC connection, on Spiritours website. Interview questions include, "What point in Spiritours philosophy touched you most? What is spirituality for you? What form does it take in your life?" The company's owner hopes to hear a candidate say, "Christian" or describe "something about a relationship with God and Jesus Christ." But in Quebec that is rare. So she tries at least not to settle for a totally self-centered, private spirituality.

Mundell & Associates reports a still more formal process that starts with reviewing jobs and developing job descriptions based on the current and projected needs of the business. Information from these tools becomes the basis for identifying a position, determining required qualifications, and provides direction on whether to advertise or connecting with a recruiter. Candidates of interest are asked to submit transcripts and complete pre-interview questionnaires which Mundell's staff then review prior to any interview. To cover some of the common, general questions, they interview multiple candidates at the same time. Later each candidate spends individual time with similar professionals at, above, and below their prospective level. Afterwards, the Mundell professionals rank the applicants. Like Dealerflow, Mundell has also been known to respond to the unexpected opportunity. Case in point: a current employee was contacted by a former colleague who was looking for work and recommended that person. At the owner's request, a small group of employees— whoever could be rounded up on short notice— interviewed the candidate to decide if he should be put through the entire process.

Among several well-thought-out aspects of Mundell's process is a pre-interview questionnaire which asks prospective candidates to articulate three things they are passionate about and requests examples of how this passion made an on-the-job difference. These questions relate, of course, to the quality the owner's preference for hiring people with a passion for the planet and engineering. In the same questionnaire candidates are asked to suggest specific ways in which Mundell might contribute to their inner motivation and to describe past mistakes or errors and what they learned from those experiences. Finally, they ask about the candidates' interest in the company and what contributions they expect to make. Because of comments about the EOC on the company's website, candidates at this point have a wide open invitation to inquire about it. When interviewers review the questionnaires and other documents, they use a five-point scale to rate candidates' technical skills, project management skills, marketing skills, consulting experience, and perceived fit.

Netuitive's full-time employees come to the company via a standardized hiring process that starts with the help of specialized recruiters who identify candidates and a security firm that performs background checks. After the recruiter has pre-filtered candidates, each is interviewed first by the hiring manager, followed by "hands-on exercises/test(s)," interviews with three or four additional team members, and finally, an interview with the CEO. While prior interviews and activities are designed to gauge a candidate's capabilities, the CEO focuses on candidates' "fit," whether they have the "DNA" that will work with the company. Are they humble? Smart? Hungry? Do they have a healthy ambition, versus just being satisfied with a position? To fit with Netuitive, says the CEO, employees need to share the same thirst for customer service, creativity and problem solving. Otherwise it will be a mismatch." How does Netuitive's CEO identify things like "humility" and "smart?" Using what he calls "proxy" questions he tries to get at openness to other ideas, customers and partners. "Do they give credit to others? How do they talk about others? How have they positioned their careers and do they give other people credit for helping them? If the CEO thinks candidates are a good fit, he will pose hypothetical ethical questions, tell them about Netuitive's values, explain what they mean, and report that people have been fired for not being able to live out those values. The candidates responses to this information is sometimes confusion, sometimes surprise, sometimes an exaggerated effort to go along with the CEO. For the CEO, the overall purpose is to get candidates to open up and talk about their own values. Afterward the CEO shares his impression with the team involved in the interview process. A positive hiring decision requires consensus by that team.[14]

---

14. Field survey interview, 2011.

Orienting New Employees

In some respects the Economy of Communion is a breathtaking idea. Individual freedom is a central dimension to the project. But how can such freedom be realized in an *institution*, a body whose very basis is predictability, uniformity, routine? By its nature, the institution seems at odds with freedom in its fullest sense. How EOC businesses cope simultaneously with the key idea of freedom and the reality of institutional constraints may be reflected in the way they introduce new employees to their businesses and its cultures. For new employees, orientation is a first experience of a new culture, a first look at what the company values actually mean and how they are practiced. There is more to orientation than training and introductions. Companies known for building and sustaining strong cultures, e.g., Medtronic, P&G or Johnson & Johnson, for example, have well-planned and extensive orientation periods. Intensive and targeted "onboarding" programs, which are used with growing frequency, seek to speed up "socialization" and help new employees become productive more quickly using various methods: e.g., meetings, videos, reading, computer-based training, and personal introductions. Even in businesses where short term employment and modest hourly pay are the norm the value of a good orientation processes is understood, e.g., Starbucks and McDonald's. So what do our EOC companies do about orienting employees? How much is the EOC mission emphasized in orientation?

Among the companies in our study, Netuitive has one of the more complete orientation programs, one that strongly reflects an "onboarding" approach. Their program includes two or three days of introductions and/or training that includes a session with the CEO to describe the company culture, vision and mission. It also includes time with human resources for the usual legal and internal forms, as well as introductions to all other employees. The new employee's respective department head also gives a presentation about roles, responsibilities and goals.

A day of "administrative" orientation at Mundell & Associates covers everything from where to get supplies to health care benefit issues. But in the environmental industry, all employees must have hazmat (safe use of materials) certification; any employee "brand new" to the business, therefore, undertakes a required and standardized 40 hour training program. New employees also get a company specific health and safety orientation. A session with the president reinforces certain critical practices and expectations. Employees hired into their first professional position also participate in job shadowing with a more experienced person. Mundell is developing orientation activities and materials that explain more about the company's vision, mission and values.

At Spiritours, a procedures book describes processes for accomplishing main tasks but also serves as the basis for training and orientation of new employees. The company takes an individualized approach to this process, customizing training to suit the individual employee's need. Departing employees are asked to train their successors, and in doing so to take time to review and update the procedures book. Other employees are also expected to give support during the training period. Spiritours' owner meets with the new employee one-on-one to explain the company's philosophy, to determine if the training has met the new employee's needs and to gauge whether he or she is "happy with the tasks and the team."

An informal approach to orientation is adequate at Dealerflow, the owner says, because the business hires so few people. The company is concerned with two things in the way it handles new employees: first getting them hands-on experience very quickly with a particular part of the software or hardware under the supervision of more than one person to give the employee good exposure to the business.

The second thing is to involve new employees quickly in team or interactive events—meetings, conferences and customer meetings. While the CEO also meets with new employees personally, the preference is to maximize mentoring and bonding, thus the focus on lots of interaction.

Finish Line conducts a "special session" to "walk through all protocols" with new consultants. The highly interactive session is geared to the needs of each individual new employee because, says Finish Line owner, everyone assimilates information in different ways. In other words, with individualized orientation Finish Line tries its best to address differences in learning styles. The focus is on giving each new person the time they need to ask questions and get them answered, to express concerns and to make suggestions. First Fruits simply relies on its "lead" student to recruit other students and to explain the business to them. Most students who show up to work on any given day, says the owner, are familiar with the company and the fact that their "business philosophy is based on Christ." Sofia Violins, which prides itself on hiring employees who require little supervision and who already seem to have the desire to make violins and to be part of the company, sees little need for formal orientation.

At some point presumably, a new employee in an EOC company is going to come across the language of EOC and want to know more about its effect on the culture. Owners vary in their thinking about whether they should formally introduce employees to the EOC connection—or even whether a formal introduction is necessary. Mundell & Associates tells prospective employees "a little bit about the fact that we are one of many businesses around the world that belong to this group. And that we share profits to help those in need," says the owner. He also reports the company's plans to incorporate more of the EOC information in his interviewing processes later. Planning for that had just begun. At Netuitive, on the other hand, EOC is not openly addressed at all because Netuitive is not technically an "EOC business." But the CEO believes that EOC values are very much a part of the environment and understood by everyone. These are the values communicated regularly by management and the values that underlie 360 degree performance reviews. Though Ideal's owner occasionally hires family members who know the EOC connection, no mention is made of it in hiring other contract associates. First Fruits make no formal mention of EOC to the college students it employs, part-time and short-term workers. For those who stay on longer, perhaps over a school year or two, "some of the 'regulars' get some introduction to EOC," but only if they ask. And when they do, she tells them as much as they want to know. For Finish Line, the situation is much the same. When people ask, says the owner, "We offer as much information as they appear to want—this could include an article or current info from around the world, anecdotes, (information) about other businesses in North America, reference to website, etc."[15] Dealerflow takes a similar approach. While the owner says he has not shared much about EOC with his staff and he is "not sure" why, he is beginning to talk about it more. "All my full timers are great Christian people and seem to appreciate what the EOC is about, even if their knowledge of it is still quite limited," he says. The owner of Arc-en-Saisons once tried to explain EOC to an employee, but, he says, it was not a success. "The EOC is hard to explain, and this employee then tried to use it against (me) by taking advantage of our relationship." Expecting "love and unity" is a challenge when an employee is not performing well, he says.[16]

In candidate interviews, Spiritours' owner tries to ask questions about some basic values that are part of the EOC. The company has a brief explanation of the EOC in their

---

15. From Survey 2, December 2008
16. From Interviews.

brochure and on their website, so applicants can read about it before they "take a step towards us," says the owner. She does talk more about the EOC when people are hired, but "I don't say too much because I want to let them discover it by themselves. I want them to take the initiative to go further and find out more." But, she adds, "With the team of our tour leaders (occasional employees), I have more courage to speak about it; maybe because I don't have to face them on a day-to-day basis." She has shown them a video and a Power Point on the subject and invited all employees to the EOC congress held in her city.[17]

Summary Observations

In some ways, the most interesting information about hiring practices in the EOC companies is what is *not* there. We saw no language about hiring to the EOC mission and no evidence of faith as a consideration in hiring. Any concerns that EOC businesses might be parochial because their mission is so rooted in the Christian tradition is not supported by our research. Hiring and orientation practices in our EOC businesses look very much like those of other small businesses. Perhaps it is a testament to the owners' sincerity in focusing on *the whole person,* not on the person's faith, religion or lack of either. Or a testament to their commitment to unity, which cannot be limited to the few, the chosen, or "people like us." It is possible—and this is not a question we probed with the owners—that the relative silence on EOC rests in concerns about driving people away. An owner who made reference to having "more courage to speak" about EOC to part-time than to full-time staff hints at such concerns.

What does come across strongly among the businesses that hire are concerns for the impact of a hire on the "team," a term that seems to be more a proxy for "community" than

17. From Survey 2, December 2008.

for actual work teams. How will this person fit into our team? What will this person add to our team? Involving "the team" in interviews and related language suggests that the owners understand the impact of hiring on the organization as a whole, and they try to get optimal hiring results by involving "the team" into the decision. In addition to clear and specific criteria related to jobs, hiring also emphasizes the person in the context of a work community. These observations suggest caution, if not reluctance, to openly promote or even discuss EOC ideas within these businesses. On the other hand, we may be observing the patience of owners who believe that "in freedom" and in Providence's own time, employees' understanding of the EOC ideal will deepen.

Chapter Six

EOC Companies:
Organizational Culture
and Leadership

"All our employees want to work for your company."[1]

We begin this chapter not with a quotation from a business expert but with a comment provided to us from a respondent. It is a comment provided to the EOC company owner by a banker with whom the owner does business. We begin this way because the quotation reflects a sentiment about EOC companies that we heard often, either directly from employees or customers or indirectly from other EOC owners. On closer examination, it is a statement about EOC company culture. The desire to work for this EOC company—in this case, a desire stated by bank employees—is created by the ongoing interaction between the bank employees and the EOC employees. The EOC employees project a welcoming attitude, and they conduct themselves in enviable ways. There is something observable and attractive in the day-to-day behavior of these employees, and we attribute that, in general, to organizational culture and leadership.

Were we to turn to organizational experts, we would find broad acceptance of the notion that culture is that aspect

---

1. From Survey 11, February 2011.

135

of a company or organization that shapes people's behavior and, in particular, shapes behavior in the absence of rules, procedures, or policies.[2] At the same time, scholars differ in their approach to the idea of organizational culture. Is it something an organization has? Or is? Views vary on the extent to which a leader shapes a culture (or culture shapes the leader), about the impact of culture on organizational performance, and—where strong cultures are associated with organizational success—which comes first, the culture or the success? Perhaps the simplest definition of culture is that offered by Terrence Deal and Allan Kennedy in their 1982 book, *Corporate Cultures: The Rites and Rituals of Corporate Life*; that is, corporate culture is "the way we do things around here."[3] More complicated definitions, such as those proposed by Edgar Schein, and found in the 1992 edition of his book, *Organizational Culture and Leadership*, recognize that culture develops over time and that it reflects group learning in response to problem solving and to success at integrating new ideas, things and people.[4] Generally speaking, culture is understood to be both perceived process and embedded content: a system of things like shared values, beliefs, symbols, and language that influence behavior. Bolman and Deal in their book, *Reframing Organizations: Artistry, Choice and Leadership* from 2008, describe culture as "the superglue that bonds an organization, unites people, and helps an enterprise accomplish desired ends."[5]

Research on organizational culture has examined normative questions about culture (e.g., whether it is strong or weak), its purported masculine or feminine character, whether it tends to shape members' behavior in similar ways,

2. Schein, Edgar., 1992. *Organizational Culture and Leadership*. San Francisco: Jossey-Bass.
3. Deal, Terrence E., and Kennedy, Allan A. 1982. *Corporate Cultures: The Rites and Rituals of Corporate Life*. Cambridge: Perseus Books..
4. Schein, p 17.
5. Bolman, Lee G., and Deal, Terrence E., 2008. *Reframing Organizations: Artistry, Choice and Leadership*. San Francisco: Jossey-Bass. p 409.

and its relationship to formalization and organizational performance. Other areas of inquiry ask whether culture can be a liability; how it begins, develops and functions; and how it can be shaped, managed, changed and kept alive. One of the most salient theoretical questions concerns the ways in which employees learn culture; that is, how are values integrated into a culture? Through symbols, language, rituals, ceremonies, stories, heroes, and heroines, and honored practices, an organization expresses and reinforces the values that give meaning to its work and community life. Culture may be as fundamental as individual choice in affecting the ethical choices and moral profile of a firm. "Ethics ultimately must be deeply rooted in soul: an organization's commitment to its deeply rooted identity, beliefs, and values,"[6] in the words of Bolman and Deal.

Of these approaches, Schein presents us with perhaps the most useful model for thinking about culture and leadership among EOC companies:

> When one brings culture to the level of the organization and even down to groups within the organization, one can see more clearly how it is created, embedded, developed, and ultimately manipulated, managed, and changed. These dynamic processes of culture creation and management are the essence of leadership and make one realize that leadership and culture are two sides of the same coin.[7]

From an evolutionary perspective, Schein argues that leaders begin to first "make" a culture from their actions, decisions, beliefs, and values, and that over time, as that culture becomes the very fabric of the organization, it begins to shape and form the actions, decisions, beliefs, and values that are acceptable and effective for the organization, including defining what constitutes acceptable leadership. Leaders, particularly in entrepreneurial enterprises, play

---

6. Bolman and Deal, p. 409.
7. Schein, p. 1.

a primary role in shaping these cultures. Their words are weighed more heavily, their actions watched more closely, and what they neglect may be as significant as to what they attend.

Schein's understanding of culture is also useful because of the conceptualization of culture as layers or "levels."[8] Organizational culture is a manifestation and an embodiment of beliefs and values, but it is not necessarily values, and almost never beliefs, that are on display. Rather the values and beliefs are only evident in the "artifacts" of culture—those things which an observer or a member of the group can see, touch, taste, smell, hear, or otherwise perceive. In an organization these certainly would include rules, policies, and procedures, but more often they include special language, symbols, logos, colors, practices, habits, discourse, meetings, and celebrations. And as Schein points out, at this level, culture is "easy to observe and very difficult to decipher."[9] Artifacts of culture are the visible manifestation of the second level of culture which is espoused and shared values, and shared beliefs.

The core of organizational culture, of any particular organization, is Schein's third level: the set of shared, basic assumptions about what's real, what's true, and what's right. These assumptions are taken for granted, but they form the bedrock, or the essence, of a group's culture. They may or may not be well articulated or even operating on a conscious plane. Understanding any particular culture, therefore, requires an attempt to uncover and understand what these basic fundamental assumptions are and how they came to be shared assumptions over time among any group. Further, any attempt to analyze culture must consider that these basic assumptions are observable in a sense by proxy. As Schein explains, shared assumptions manifest

---

8. Schein, p. 17.
9. Ibid.

themselves at the most observable level, as artifacts, and at a more subtle level of espoused and shared values, norms, and rules of behavior. The original source of the shared, basic assumptions is leadership.

Leadership is originally the source of the beliefs and values that get a group moving in dealing with its internal and external problems. If what a leader proposes works and continues to work, what once was only the leader's assumption gradually comes to be a shared assumption.[10]

Schein's model presents us with a useful approach for analysis. In seeking data about the culture of our subject EOC companies, we asked open-ended questions about "artifacts" and about values. Our task then was to attempt to "decipher" the culture of these EOC companies. Reflecting on this task for a moment, we should mention that we already know there are espoused EOC values; the EOC and the Focolare are intentional about inculcating the larger society with a certain spirituality, a certain practice, and a certain way of living.

We first elaborated on these EOC and Focolare values in our opening chapter. Schein's model suggests there might be a certain degree of uniformity among the cultures of EOC companies. Certainly, there exists a uniformity of basic assumptions and espoused values, but to what extent might artifacts be uniform? How many different ways can closely held, similar, beliefs and values be manifest? Certainly the company leaders we know espoused certain shared EOC and Focolare values, but how uniform can we expect their approach be to inculturating these values? Taking a cue from Schien's model, we asked about stories, celebrations, traditions, special language, and symbols, and also about mission and vision statements. Generally, these are questions about what Schein refers to as the artifacts

---

10. Schein, p 27.

of culture.[11] In that process we are seeking to uncover the values manifest in those artifacts.

We then asked specific questions about values, particularly the values that are or might be explicitly embedded in formal statements. In other words, this is where, presumably, the owner has set out to articulate and promulgate those values. We also asked about *whether* and *how* those values are otherwise known to employees and customers. In other words, if an owner has not set out to explicitly articulate values in some sort of values statement, then how do employees become aware of the organization's values? We also were able to discover some things about this in our conversations with employees. What follows is our examination of both the embedded content and processes of culture (the artifacts and manifest values), followed by a closer look at leadership and the process of inculturation.

The EOC Take on Culture

Let's begin with what we learned from employees of the EOC companies. In general, the culture of these companies is described by employees as *open* and *respectful*. What they mean by "open" is a non-judgmental, welcoming culture that is accepting of the ideas, feelings, opinions, and expertise of others. Employees are engaged with each other and genuinely interested in each other. They care about each other's lives and not just about work. Several of these companies have been described by employees as friendlier and less stressful than other places of employment. One employee described his organization as "more a person business than a money business."[12] Another employee remarked, "There is joy here."[13] But "open" also means an attitude toward communication marked by interaction, collaboration, cooperation, high energy, and very intentional

---

11. Ibid.
12. From Field Study Interviews, June 2010.
13. Ibid.

and pervasive transparency. At Spiritours, for example, this openness and respect is expressed through such practices as taking the time to insure that "everything is explained" to both clients and employees.[14] At Netuitive, an open and respectful culture includes open-book management, where financial and other performance data is shared. Employees at Netuitive readily acknowledge that it is incumbent on everyone to be transparent and to hold each other account-able. They insist on honest, open communication and on facing conflict head-on without politics or "gamesmanship" so that everyone gets better at the work that they do.[15] They emphasize that this promotes open engagement, high levels of preparation, sensitivity to not wasting people's time, and readily available feedback, all of which contribute to the accomplishment of significant things.

Our EOC companies also appear to manifest some of the same cultural attributes toward customers, and this is observed and recognized by customers. As one employee of Mundell & Associates says, "If customers had a description of EOC that was crisp, clear and concise, they would rec-ognize the connection."[16] Mundell & Associates, Spiritours, Netuitive, First Fruits, Arc-en-Saisons, Finish Line, Terra Nuova, and CHB all work very hard to convey to customers what they will or will not do as well as what they can and cannot do (in terms of capabilities). These companies make an effort to represent their products or services honestly, transparently, and clearly, and to expect this of employees. In short, the cultures of these companies are remarkably similar. There is a willingness and an openness to talk about values. There is certainly a reliance on stories and storytelling, celebrations, and some traditions; conversely, there is very little reliance on overly formal mission state-ments, vision statements, symbols, or language.

---

14. Ibid.
15. Ibid.
16. From Field Interviews, Spring 2008.

One inescapable and obvious conclusion is that these companies are *storytellers*. They are full of stories: stories about each other; stories about their foibles and follies; stories about the meaningful and significant events in the life of the company; stories about accomplishments, about work well done, about satisfied customers. Typical of these stories are those from La Parola, Finish Line, and Sofia—stories in which divine providence seems to be almost immediate and miraculous. The owner of Sofia, for instance, tells one story about needing to call a list of delinquent customers, but he was sidetracked by the needs of an immigrant employee who was about to buy a house but without a clue as to how to complete the application process. The owner of Sofia put off calling delinquent customers in order to spend the entire day helping the employee. Unnoticed at first, but confirmed later, was the fact that while everyone's attention was focused on helping the employee, a full payment from every delinquent customer arrived in that day's mail.

La Parola can tell similar stories about the providential arrival of funds, and Finish Line can tell the story of six needed students showing up within 30 minutes of the company praying for such a blessing. Spiritours tells the story of the hiring of its first employee, who insisted on working without pay simply for the chance to be a part of the company. But there are more complex stories that suggest a deeper sensitivity to the working of providence even when providence takes a long time to reveal its course. Mundell & Associates, for example, is often able to connect certain pieces of current business to events and circumstances that occurred well in the past. The company fondly relates the story of a Saturday several years ago, when all employees and their spouses came together to do some rehab work at an inner-city housing project. The effort resulted in some unexpected coverage by a TV news crew and also introduced some of the spouses to the capabilities and ideals of the company. The increased visibility and awareness gained from that single day continues to provide business opportunities today. Mundell & Associates certainly reads this as providential.

While it is hard to <u>overstate</u> the importance of storytelling to EOC companies, it is hard to <u>understate</u> the importance of formal mission and vision statements. This is not because mission, vision, and values are not important. Rather, it is the *formality* that eludes EOC companies. This, of course, is not uniformly the case. Mundell & Associates, for example, is hard at work on formal mission, vision, and values statements. In fact, these exist already, but the company is in the midst of efforts to refine and improve them.

But why might formal mission statements matter? Much is made in the strategy literature about the purpose and value of formal mission statements. In fact, some argue that strategic management begins with the creation of a formal mission statement or, more specifically, when an organization defines its mission.[17] In their classic study, *Built to Last: Successful Habits of Visionary Companies*, Jim Collins and Jerry Porras identified a number of visionary companies for whom everything is defined in and by their mission statement. Included among these companies are American Express, Procter & Gamble, IBM, Merck, Ford, General Electric and Disney, to name a few. The important thing here is the evidence that visionary firms with such mission centrality enjoy better than average performance even though profit maximization or economic performance is not a central part of that mission.[18] There is a substantial

---

17. Peter Drucker is among the most convincing management experts when it comes to the value of mission, suggesting that is among the more difficult questions that companies must come to terms with, and describing it as the first responsibility of strategists. Peter Drucker, 1974. *Management; Tasks, Responsibilities, and Practices,* New York: Harper & Row. p 61.

18. Collins, Jim and Porras, Jerry I. 2004. *Built to Last: Successful Habits of Visionary Companies.* New York: HarperBusiness.

body of studies that suggests formalized mission statements enhance firm performance.[19]

Proponents of formalized mission statements generally see them as providing a standard or a benchmark against which the organization can develop specific objectives, measure progress, evaluate performance, and allocate resources. But beyond these common uses, proponents also argue that formal mission statements provide a sense of identity and unified purpose, a standard for individual and collective behavior, and a rubric for strategic formulation and revision.[20] Why, then, might EOC companies appear reticent to embrace these significant benefits? It may be that the conventional wisdom about mission statements is not useful or relevant to the EOC. The EOC company is trying first to act in a certain way to accomplish or be something more than shared purpose around a product or service. In other words, would developing a conventional mission statement be a way of settling for something less—of settling, in a sense, for mediocrity? Would it divert time, energy, and attention away from the more important tasks and considerations?

Let us turn our attention back to Mundell & Associates, and consider first their mission statement:

> To bring our experiences, education, creativity, talents, personalities and group synergy together to support our clients in solving their most difficult earth science and environmental challenges. We do this using the most state-of-the-art technologies to achieve technically-sound, cost-effective and sustainable solutions that respect the environment.

---

19. Rarick, Charles and Vitton, John. 1995. "Mission Statements Make Cents," *Journal of Business Strategy*, 16. And also Bart, Christopher and Baetz, Mark. 1998. "The relationship between Mission Statements and Firm Performance: An Exploratory Study," *Journal of Management Studies* 35.
20. King, W.R. and Cleland D.I. 1979, *Strategic Planning and Policy*. NewYork: Van Nostrand Reinhold. p 124.

By almost all measures, this mission statement goes a long way toward accomplishing the typical objectives of formal mission statements; it answers the question: What is our business? However, also revealing is the concomitant vision statement, which attempts to answer the question: What do we want to become?

> *We consider communication to be a gift of self, and view open and honest communication as a foundation of the trust that we build with each other, and of the integrity with which we perform our work. The fruit of that trust is honesty and sharing of ideas without fear.*
>
> *We value and nurture our relationships with each other, with our customers, suppliers, partners, and all with whom we work. We find ways to enjoy working together, and to celebrate each other's successes as well as to support each other in times of difficulty.*
>
> *As a people-centered organization, we work together to meet the needs of our customers, while giving back to society and to our local communities with the well-being of others and the common good in mind. We look for ways to perform works of charity and care to all those with whom we come in contact in concrete ways.*[21]

Some of this language is clearly inspired by EOC and Focolare values—"gift of self," "works of charity"—and while some other parts of the language are less obviously EOC inspired, it is still language that speaks more to the existence of a group of persons in some kind of relationship than to the existence of a group of people that share some common purpose around a product or service. This is a vision statement that might serve to remind employees of the

---

21. From Survey 11, February 2010.

focus on relationship rather than on conventional aspects of business.

Although Mundell & Associates stands out among our respondent companies for these efforts to formalize and articulate the values that drive the organization, all the EOC companies we surveyed are readily open, articulate, and explicit about their values. These values include love, service, listening, and sharing (La Parola); real actions, as in the Focolare ideal of living it first, then speaking it (Mundell & Associates); honesty; that we are all one family; universal brotherhood; mutual respect; the innate dignity, uniqueness, originality, and identity of each person; responsibility; the awareness that each person makes a difference (Finish Line and Spiritours); relationship capital (CHB); and the glory of God (First Fruits).

These values are evident in their celebrations, for, in addition to storytelling, EOC companies make serious use of celebrations. They celebrate like families: birthdays, Christmas, weddings, anniversaries, and births. And they celebrate as friends: client and employee successes, new employees, departing employees, new certifications or achievements, and professional and personal achievements. And like family and friends, they gather for funerals and illnesses, particularly those requiring hospitalization. Company social events often involve employees' families, e.g., the Memorial Day picnic, a trip to the zoo, or a baseball game. But they make little use of symbols or special language.

Netuitive has created their culture by doing, by acting. Netuitive employees speak first about the value placed on the widespread sharing of knowledge and information within the company. They use the word transparency to describe this, but it seems to us to be much more. Transparency implies being able to see through a "veil" of some sort. At Netuitive, there appears to be no veil; employees claim they "dare to tell the truth about each other."[22] And the absence of a veil pervades other activities, such as internal engineering, the establishment of work plans and deadlines, and telling customers what they will not or cannot do.[23] Netuitive looks to set fairly precise timetables, and so employees do not accept from themselves vague or unrealistic project due dates.

Leadership and Profit Distribution

What, then, do these cultural attributes say about the leadership of these EOC companies? First, these leaders, not unlike other leaders, are *actors*; they are *doers* first and talkers later. The EOC company leader demonstrates through his or her actions that the intention, the purpose and the aspiration of the company is to accomplish or be something more than merely a shared purpose around a product or service.

Since leaders according to Schein "make a culture through their actions, decisions, beliefs, and values" as we argued near the beginning of this chapter, we wanted to investigate one of the more intriguing questions about the EOC: the question of profit distribution. This is one of the characteristics of the EOC that raises eyebrows during explanations to those unfamiliar with the project. And as we mentioned early on, one of the things that captured our attention about the EOC is the commitment to share profits with those in need. Thus, here is one aspect of EOC business practice that clearly lies at the intersection of culture, values, and leadership, and might then offer some revelation about EOC leadership decisions, beliefs, and values.

---

22. From Field Study Interviews, April 2010.
23. According to Netuitive employees, the founder of the company is fond of encouraging customers to specifically "ask if we can do this for you" so that he can emphatically tell them no, and thereby clarify what the company can do, but also what it cannot. This forces the company to be clear about its capabilities but also serves to clarify customer expectations.

To accomplish this examination, though, we have to first present some additional context about the EOC understanding of profit distribution.

The current description of this on the EOC website is as follows:

> *The businesses are the pillar of the project. They freely commit themselves to put their profits in common, dividing them into three parts with the following corresponding goals:*

> *Support the development of persons and communities that find themselves in need, through shared projects based on reciprocity, subsidiarity and communion;*

> *Spread the culture of giving and of reciprocity, a pre-condition to integral development and of an economy and society characterized by fraternity and solidarity;*

> *Development of the business, creating jobs and wealth, orienting all internal and external business life towards the common good.*[24]

And here is how we described it in Chapter 1:

> One part of profits must be reserved for reinvestment in the business to support capacity for efficiency, competitiveness and sustainability. A second part would go EOC to be used in common for activities that promoted a "culture of giving" and advanced the work of EOC itself. The final share of profits, to be held by EOC in common, would be reserved for job creation and meeting material needs of those who share a belief in the spirit of the project.[25]

---

24. http://www.edc-online.org/en/eoc/the-communion-of-goods.html. Retrieved on July 22, 2014
25. This is from their current website (http://www.edc-online.org/), and as written in Chapter 1. Retrieved July 22, 2014.

We are concerned here about a three-part distribution of profits: one, to reinvest in the business; two, to spread the "culture of giving"; and three, to share with those in need. Two further points must be made: first, all of our surveyed EOC company owners take a salary out of the expenses of the business. We don't know how much. One thing that seems prevalent and clear is that there are no additional distributions of cash to the owners beyond the salary. At least one owner is putting money away for retirement. Second, there is no formal requirement or prescription involved here. There is no EOC audit, there is no coercion, there is no report that must be filed with anyone, and neither the EOC nor the Focolare do any checking up on this. This is what they mean by the Economy of Communion in Freedom.

But what does all this really mean in the life of a business—in the day-to-day life? How does this play out in the face of the daily realities of managing a company? In part, these questions are fueled by the abstract language with which these commitments are articulated. In part, they also are fueled by our awareness of the complexities and intricacies of business life, including the decision-making process inherent even in the preparation and publication of financial statements and tax returns and the determination of investments and expenses. Included among these complexities are the determination of compensation to the business owner and other employees and the specific treatment of questions about "corporate donations" or "corporate philanthropy" and their effects on profits and taxes.

It seemed to us that these queries about distribution of profit were questions of organizational culture and leadership, particularly since the answers reveal a great deal about strategic vision, direction and imagination. At the same time, these are questions of the utmost practical and tactical kind. How much investment is really required in the business, and how are those decisions made? For us, these decisions are undeniably and inescapably matters of leadership. Decisions about these very important questions are being made in some fashion by some person or persons in the company and are therefore a crucial piece of the EOC business practices puzzle.

We asked about this, and here is what we learned:

> The actual decision making in this arena appears to be highly centralized; that is to say, the decision is in the province and purview of the business owner.

If there is a discernible pattern among EOC companies with respect to timing, it is that most make specific profit redistribution decisions on an annual basis, coinciding with the end of each calendar year or tax year. Several of the companies make a profit redistribution decision twice a year, specifically mentioning June and December.

Collectively, the approach to decision making here seems to be careful and cautious but at the same time infused with generosity. The caution stems from the concrete realization that the sustainability of the business is paramount. Several of our EOC owners point out the inherent futility of giving everything away, endangering the health of the business, and becoming needy themselves. This was put to us in exactly the same way by almost everyone—to the point that it was obvious they have shared substantive discussion and agreement about this pragmatic approach. "We can't become the needy,"[26] is how the owner of Spiritours puts it. Similarly, they know they cannot give so much cash away in one time period that they may be forced to borrow cash in a future time period. One owner, in fact, has been building a cash reserve since the business was founded.

But this caution of not becoming the needy is coupled with generosity. Finish Line, for example, does their best to estimate future investment needs—based on known possibilities—and then sends all the remaining profits off to

---

26. From Focus Group conversations, August 2009.

Rome. So, too, do La Parola and First Fruits. Many companies give all that they can give. Others make a point to give
twice a year, driven by the recognition that the needs of the
people they are trying to serve do not necessarily march in
time to the company's fiscal year.

When we explored the second tenets of EOC profit
redistribution—i.e. spreading the culture of giving—we
learned that EOC owners may not clearly distinguish or
even recognize some of their activities as fulfilling this te-
net. For example, all of these business owners involve their
companies in local community efforts. This might include
activities ranging from sponsorship of youth activities and
programming to a community volunteer day. Such activities could certainly be interpreted as a way of spreading the
culture of giving. Moreover, these sponsorships or community involvement events are being paid for from corporate
revenues, so technically, they reduce profits and are a type
of "profit redistribution." However, most EOC owners did
not readily suggest their community activities as examples
of profit redistribution or spreading the culture of giving.

Here's another example: the activities and expenses
related to involvement in the EOC community. All of the
business owners participate more fully and broadly in the
EOC project and in the broader life of the Focolare. As EOC
business owners they are in collaboration with each other.
They participate in the regional annual meeting of the EOC,
which at the time of this writing includes the United States
and Canada. They are also active in the local churches and
in the local Focolare activities. Activities that are unquestionably EOC-related—such as attendance in the annual
meeting and occasional travel to other meetings or speaking engagements as EOC participants—are usually paid for
out of company expenses. (This is not the case for the one
company which is not an EOC-owner company but whose
CEO is an EOC and a Focolare participant, but even he says
that if he owned an EOC company he would do it this way.)

In this sense, the companies pay for EOC involvement. At the same time, there are activities that EOC business owners undertake themselves. This might include speaking to schools and universities and being active in the local community. One of the businesses, Mundell & Associates, was led to create an international internship program that allows young people from around the world to work for a time in an EOC company somewhere else in the world. Needless to say, these activities involve some expenses that are picked up by the company. This reduces profits, at least Profit &Loss profits or accounting profits, in our language. We think this could be viewed as a redistribution of profits. But to what extent did EOC owners recognize their EOC activities as spreading the culture of giving? Interestingly, not all business owners had thought about it in these terms. In fact, our question seemed to catch them by surprise. Clearly, when it comes to the EOC commitment to profit redistribution and spreading the culture of giving, most EOC companies limit their conscious decisions in this regard to their cash donations and do not factor in their other contributions to their community and their EOC involvement, despite how remarkable these contributions are.

Summary Observations

Let's work backward through this chapter, beginning with our discussion about leadership and profit distribution. First, it is noteworthy that decisions about profits are largely centralized and the exclusive province of the company founder or owner. That is to say, there isn't any sort of company-wide rubric or meeting or established procedure to involve other members of the companies in the actual decision. There does seem to be some effort to engage other members of the organization in determining what the reinvestment needs might be, but there are no discussions about alternative uses for profits, say for bonuses, pay increases,

additional benefits, or the like. Profit redistribution decisions are, therefore, quite singular and generally reserved
within the province of the owner.

There is a possible puzzle here. There is certainly a
high regard for persons apparent in the artifacts of EOC
company culture, and in many cases, explicit, but often
informal, articulation of the value placed on persons and
relationships, but at the same time, decisions about profit
redistribution tend to exclude others. From a leadership
perspective, it can be argued that full and open participation
in profit redistribution decisions are both an opportunity to
further reinforce important values (and therefore strengthen
the culture) AND an opportunity to put those values into
practice in the same way they are put into practice in regard
to communication and celebration. Further, from a leadership perspective, most EOC business owners don't seem
to readily recognize or interpret the myriad ways in which
they are, in effect, spreading the culture of giving. None of
the business owners seem to view the management of their
companies as in any way a manifestation of spreading the
culture of giving.

What is clear, however, is that EOC leadership reflects a
pragmatic generosity fueled by a dependence on providence.
There is an acute awareness that they shouldn't give away so
much that they ruin the business, become the needy, or are
forced into borrowing money, yet there are several owners
who gladly give away everything they can over and above
identified, concrete needs. This conviction about providence, in fact, might be the bedrock of their culture. The
EOC explicitly, consciously, intentionally, and deliberately
acts in a way that suggests that providential intervention is
imminent. This is really an active expression of a profound
sense of hope. It is not a distancing of self from a thorny or
an apparently insoluble matter and just tossing it into God's
hands. It is recognition that divine intervention is possible
everywhere and anywhere, every time and any time, with

everyone and anyone. Further, EOC companies tell stories all the time because they believe that it's quite likely that there will be some future connected event to the story. So, they tell themselves stories as a way of not forgetting, as a way of anticipating the future. They want to remember incidences and experiences because they expect it will return to them in some way, shape or form, bringing with it a witness that they are all in this together, that they are reliant on a providential intervention.

The artifacts of an EOC culture, therefore, include openness, honesty, respect, transparency, genuine engagement with others, joy, stories, and celebrations. Cultural values include a deep respect for other persons and a profound emphasis on the primacy of relationships. There exists a common commitment to the ideals of the EOC and a conscious, intentional, pervasive, and ongoing search for ways to live out that commitment and to examine their business practices in light of those ideals. As leaders, EOC owners generally favor action over talk and certainly have been instrumental in imbuing their organizational cultures with their values and ideals (and fundamental beliefs and assumptions), with the possible exception of the profit distribution arena. It remains to be seen where and how EOC business owners will grapple with this in the future.

Chapter Seven

EOC Companies:
Their Defining Moments

Defining moments shape an organization because they cut through all of the finely crafted
pronouncements about what the company as-
pires to do and reveal instead what it actually
does.[1]

At some point in this investigation, it was inevitable
that we would seek to uncover how a business
owner reacted to, and dealt with challenges. For in some
areas of business, as in life, behavior can and is shaped by
routine, by habit, by practice, by tradition, by policy. In business, it is, or can be, well and good to have approaches to
marketing, or human resources, that are prescribed; to have
routines and repetitive practices that flow from values, and
that result in some consistency that in time results in some
identifiable way of doing business on a recurring basis. But
then there are defining moments.

These are the events and circumstances that are unforeseen and unexpected, and where our responses, our actions,
and our behavior cannot be rehearsed; where there is no
policy, no habit, no past practice to fall back on. These reveal the heart and soul of a company. This hearkens back to
what we said in Chapter One in our discussion of Selznick's

---

1. Badaracco, Joseph L., Jr. 1997. *Defining Moments: When Managers Must Choose
between Right and Right.* Boston: Harvard Business School Press, p 64.

ideas about organizational behavior that is responsive and adaptive. Here we quote from Selznick:

> As an organization evolves it learns from experience, encounters the unexpected, discovers challenges that must be faced, and does not deny the reality that things happen which are neither planned nor foreseeable. As the organization finds ways to respond and adapt, those ways eventually become shared, habitual behavior. The phenomenon of responsiveness and adaptation are shared within the organization. Individual responses and adaptations are "values" driven because there is the possibility for people to act in concert with the values they hold, and with what they believe to be true or right. The responses are neither random nor illogical; a discernible pattern reveals itself.[2]

It is no different for our EOC companies. They have moments when values are tested, tempered, sometimes forged for the first time. They have moments when they perhaps learn about themselves what they did not already know, or even suspect. These are the times when they come face-to-face with whatever prior hypothetical speculation they may have engaged in.

Badarocco's book is largely about leadership and "defining moments" in the context of individual managerial behavior. He rightly calls attention to what is at stake for an individual manager, and argues that managers are often faced with decisions between right and right; that is, where several courses of action or decision could possibly be right or moral. For the individual manager these decisions reveal basic and fundamental values. Moreover, they reveal how committed the manager is to values that they espouse. And, these decisions shape the manager—they cannot be undone, and their consequences leave an imprint of the life of the manager. Each defining moment in essence holds the

---

2. Perrow, p 158.

manager's life in a balance—from henceforth, the manager's life will not be the same. Defining moments than are life-changing events; or, as the phrase implies, life defining.

Badaracco also recognizes though that it is not possible to separate these defining moments in the life of an individual manager from the life of the organization to which the manager belongs. "Defining moments are social as well as personal."[3] In fact, according to Badaracco, this phenomenon highlights the "most challenging and creative elements of the work of business leaders: adapting, interpreting, and customizing basic human values in a way that guides and shapes an entire company."[4]

We asked our business owners to talk about these challenging and creative elements at three different times in our investigation. We were conducting this research just as the financial meltdown and the economic recession were beginning in late 2008. In the spring of 2009, we asked them to reflect on how the recession was affecting their business and their company, and how they were responding. Later, we asked them, in an open-ended way, to reflect on challenges—the most significant challenges they had faced as a business—the most significant business challenges. And finally, we asked them to reflect specifically on ethical challenges.

The defining moments experienced by these companies are—at the end of the day—no different from the defining moments and challenging experiences that confront any and all businesses. They are the challenges of business. They are the challenges of competition, the challenges of being in relationship to customers, to employees, and to other stakeholders. They might be perceived as ethical challenges or economic challenges, or relationship challenges, but there is clearly no immunity from them for the EOC. The balance

---

3. Badaracco, p 63.
4. Badaracco, p 64.

of this chapter discusses the types of challenges reported by
our companies, and then presents specific responses to, and
the personal and organizational changes wrought by, those
challenges. Following this is an exploration of our business
owners' reflections on their guiding principles in the face of
challenge, and then our own observations and reflections.

A Litany of Challenges

Although only one of our subject companies identified
their most significant challenges as associated with the
economic downturn of 2008 (the "Great Crisis of 2008"),[5]
eight of them reported substantive impacts on their business stemming from the economic downturn. Thus, on the
face of it, a clear majority of our companies have faced
and endured the economic downturn in much the same
fashion as other companies, large and small, all over the
world. EOC companies are certainly not immune to the
same economic pressures as everyone else. But these are,
by no means, the pressures they view as their most significant challenges. Among the eight companies that reported
effects on their business from the recession, these usually
involved their customers, suppliers, and competitors. Seven
reported a detrimental effect on sales but only four reported
a concomitant negative effect on profits and, of these, only
two reported an outright negative effect on their longer-
term growth prospects. One of these companies, Netuitive,
suffered negative effects on both sales and profits, and on
future growth prospects in some customer segments, but
they were also able to report (as we'll explore below) that
their response resulted in unanticipated growth in other
customer segments that quickly provided offsetting gains

5. The global meltdown in the financial services and banking industry that began in late
    2007 and triggered a contraction of global economic activity throughout 2008 and
    into 2009 and continuing even today has been labeled many things; the Great Reces-
    sion, the great financial crisis, the Recession of 2008, The Meltdown, the Crash, etc.
    Our phrase of choice, The Great Crisis of 2008, comes from Ghemawat, Pankaj *2011*,
    World 3.0, Boston: Harvard Business School Press.

in both sales and profits. For several companies, the drop in sales and/or profits was quite severe. For La Parola, the number of clients fell by 73%. For Terra Nuova, business volume declined by 30%, and for Sofia Violins, the drop was 17%. Netuitive's sales to the financial sector fell by half almost immediately. CHB Associates only reports that sales were "greatly affected,"[6] but that one client went bankrupt and that their income subsequently dropped.

Despite negative economic effects stemming from the recession, the dominant challenges these companies face come from the competitive environment. The most noteworthy challenges are those that arise in the normal course of competition; either common industry practices or generally common business and competitive practices. Netuitive, for example, operates in a high-tech software industry and consequently deals with intellectual property issues. They, and their competitors, are typically given access to confidential customer information and proprietary databases. So for them, the use and abuse of confidential information is a perennial challenge. They encounter competitors who routinely resort to spreading fear, uncertainty, and doubt about competitor capabilities and propensities.

Other challenges encountered in the competitive arena include underbidding by competitors who are anxious to land a contract or be awarded a job, "trash talking" competitors, and efforts by competitors to steal employees away often by overpromising prospective benefits. Spiritours and Mundell & Associates both face opportunities where they collaborate with competitors and must deal with the challenge of the integrity of those competitors. In the environmental services and consulting industry, Mundell & Associates must deal with competitors who purposefully underbid projects or underpay employees in order to land contracts.

---

6. From Survey 5, June 2009.

Customers, too, can present specific challenges. Mundell
& Associates, again, encounters customers who occasionally withhold payments from a contract (the check is in the
mail) or soliciting bids for work they know is already going
to a particular contractor and giving contractors' information about bids so they can bid the lowest and win the job.
In a similar vein, they encounter customers who are simply
after the lowest price and are willing to make compromises
for that (in ethics, or service) and customers who ask for
what competitors have promised. For example, a competitor
may have told a prospective customer that a certain feature
or service can be provided at a certain price and then customers start demanding that of all bidders. There are some
customers who might make a political contribution a de
facto requirement for landing a particular piece of business
and some customers with widely divergent values from the
company owner.

Efforts to grow amidst competition also present somewhat normal challenges. Finish Line worked hard to open a
second facility in the midst of the economic downturn and,
at the same time, lost the service and experience of one of
the company's founding members (to illness). They were
therefore faced with such evolving challenges as training
new consultants, and developing additional course offerings. And, as we might expect, the process of competition
for First Fruits forces them to deal with weather related
challenges, seasonally adjusted maintenance programs,
flooding, water erosion, and fire hazard possibilities, and
plant and animal diseases that require vet work and spray-
ing and pruning. Netuitive has encountered prospective
new employees who offer to provide inside or confidential
information from their previous employer. Often this is
information that has been stolen and may include competitive secrets or proprietary and confidential information or
customer contacts.

Clearly though, the most significant challenges faced by our EOC companies are those that are embedded in the relationships with their own employees. Netuitive relates an episode about a sales rep that they had terminated from their company for nonperformance where after a few months, they began to see two signs that the terminated sales rep had gone to work for another company, an aspiring competitor. First, the rep's new employer was appearing as competition in most of their bidding and second, emails from that company began appearing in a non-public inbox. That email address could only be available to someone outside the company if it had been stolen. Netuitive's suspicions proved to be correct. The terminated sales rep had stolen their customer database, shared their sales forecast with the new employer and legal action was necessary to stop this infringement. The legal action resulted in the former sales rep losing this new job, and the new employer dispatching forensic experts to make sure that the unauthorized information had really been destroyed.

Mundell & Associates, too, has found employee-related issues to be the most challenging. The owner related the particularly painful experience of a senior employee who was once very highly regarded. But as the company grew, the employee' aptitude and skills failed to grow. Shortcomings in the ability to supervise other employees, to adhere to schedules and budgets, and to achieve goals became apparent. As the employee's performance deteriorated, the employee was shifted from a supervisory role to a more consultative role. This engendered significant resentment and the employee eventually left the company and went to work for a competitor. After a period of a few months, the former employee recruited away other Mundell & Associates employees with the promise of higher salaries. Eventually, however, this once highly regarded Mundell & Associates employee was let go from the second employer while the recruited employees remained.

Finish Line has dealt with two management team members moving from New York to Texas, forcing them to establish a remote reception center that allowed phone calls to be answered from Texas, and to create an electronic computer log that allowed all necessary and pertinent information about billing, calls from customers, appointments, and inquiries to be shared across the company regardless of geography. They also have dealt with employee life-threatening illnesses, and board members with no prior EOC experience.

There is one episode involving employee related challenges that we would like to relate verbatim. It comes from Sofia Violins, and it stems partly from managing a critical subsidiary that is halfway around the world. The only editing of this story is to leave the country name blank.

> Of the many serious challenges our company has faced over the years, I immediately think of the last days of our subsidiary company in ＿＿ It was a company we set up over twenty years ago to participate in our musical instrument production-sharing operation. For decades our employees were among the best paid people in their country. A couple of years ago, the woman who had managed the operation decided she wanted even more money … as a "pension". She stopped sending any financial reports, etc., leaving us totally in the dark as we continued to send thousands of dollars for rent, salaries, taxes and other expenses every month. She was eventually dismissed. In response, she broke into our workshop late one night and stole $45,000 worth of finished product. Because of a rather corrupt legal system there was no recourse possible to recover the instruments.
>
> We quickly made the decision to exit ＿＿ We attempted to do it in a way that would give our employees the possibility of continuing their work. We gave them all of the company's equipment and years of cured production wood material. We told them that we could be their largest customer. (We called it a "Happy Birthday ESOP".) In response, our past

employees immediately began contacting our customers to see if they could get them away from us. In doing so, they blatantly infringed on our trademark. For us, that was the end of any contact with them.[7]

Beyond employee related matters, several of our companies have been, and are, challenged by legal battles, and by regulatory issues, particularly involving environmental regulations or taxation questions. Spiritours, for example, was drawn into defamation litigation by a former employed consultant who also owed the company money. The lawsuit was without merit and construed by Spiritours as an avenue being pursued to avoid payment, but it nevertheless presented her with a rather public challenge to the company's reputation. First Fruits particularly faces challenges in the environmental arena finding that expansion possibilities such as starting a dairy, fruit processing, farm tour or retail operation are made unaffordable by the time and money required for necessary permits and approvals and the accompanying impact studies and required mitigations. Even in their current business, they face challenges due to weather and to natural resource constraints, such as water, that are subject to use regulation. Taxation challenges face those companies that operate in a prevailing culture that condones cash payments to employees and under reporting of income in order to avoid taxation. Spiritours and Arc-en-Saisons both were advised by professionals at the startup phase of their companies to take certain steps to avoid taxation.

Responding to Challenges

As we might expect, facing and resolving these business challenges brings change. This is a normal dynamic in business and exactly the process that Selznick describes — organizations face challenges, resolve the challenges, and

---

7. From Survey 10, December, 2009.

discover in that process their core values. Those values then are instrumental in facing future challenges. And so companies grow and become institutionalized. And, we find this over and over again. The response to specific challenges is revealing in and of itself. Let's examine several of these and then turn our attention to responses that in fact changed these companies.

The CHB owner sometimes finds himself ending a relationship because he really can't ethically, morally, and personally support the values of a client. And, this is not for lack of effort. One client, in particular (the company's largest), had been a client for years and increasingly resisted the guidance and recommendations provided by CHB about human resources and financial practices. Ultimately CHB decided to resign the account and walk away from the revenue, explaining this as a matter of conformance to personal values.

La Parola has been asked to refund customers even after these customers have availed themselves of services. Again, in one instance, a customer demanded a refund, received it, but later returned it with the explanation that the customer was simply conducting a test of the owner's integrity. Mundell & Associates receives invitations to political fund-raisers often during the time period when the political entities are in the bid review, decision-making phase. The company's stance of not attending fund-raisers (while occasionally making small contributions) has led to not receiving contracts. But it has also led to new business from clients familiar with and supportive of their practice. Arc-en-Saisons deals with employees who insist on being paid under the table and in cash so as to avoid taxation, but avoids the practice and pays full taxes as required by local law, as does Spiritours. First Fruits responds to regulatory challenges by speaking out at public meetings and by voting for public servants with a pro-business stance. The defamation lawsuit involving Spiritours (mentioned above) was resolved when the owner sent the plaintiff a conciliatory but demanding email, also copied to every-one in the professional association for that industry. They finally resolved the suit and got paid, but then discovered they had been overpaid. The owner thought about keeping the overpayment as compensation, but ultimately made the decision in the spirituality of unity to view restitution of that overpayment as an act of humility.

In each of these examples, we find EOC companies walk-ing away from business, scrupulously following regulations, cheerfully (sometimes reluctantly) refunding payments, participating in the civic process while avoiding attempts at undue influence, making restitution where appropriate, and looking to reconcile with detractors.

Not surprisingly, the economic downturn did force most of our companies into making some changes — some small, some quite strategic. What is a bit surprising though is that two companies were able to report some significant changes made prior to the recession, both born of opportunity that proved to be prescient. That is, that led to circumstances that proved helpful in weathering the downturn. One com-pany is Sofia Violins, the other is Spiritours. Sofia tells their story best:

> A few months prior to this economic downturn, however, we made some major changes in our overhead expenses that proved to be a significant contributor to our stability. These were cost saving decisions that could not have been better timed. Providentially, we had carefully downsized our com-pany in advance of the recession. For example: ...Three years ago we moved our company from "fancy" quarters to a very nice but less elegant location. The move saved us thousands of dollars a year. And then, for twenty years we owned our own subsidiary company. In 2008 we gave the company with its equipment and thousands of dollars in aged material to our employees. With all of the overhead costs and, unfor-tunately, staff dishonesty, we decided it would be more cost

effective to simply buy the finished product from them and Western European associates.[8]

In a similar vein, Spiritours had done two things just prior to the downturn. One, they had offered ten new tours and printed the brochure and sales literature announcing those tours, and two, they had initiated a new relationship with a collaborator—someone in the travel business who was cross-marketing their tours with some of her own services. The outcome, given the downturn, was that five of the ten new tours had to be cancelled because of insufficient demand, but the relationship with the new collaborator resulted in selling an additional five new tours. Thus, essentially, the effect of the downturn was neutral.

In addition to these, Finish Line moved ahead with plans to open another tutoring facility, Netuitive quickly moved toward selling other market segments and also selling software packages with a smaller "footprint" and therefore a lower price point and entry point for new customers in those segments, and Mundell & Associates moved to adopting a more frugal attitude. For all five of these companies, then, the response to the economic downturn was, in effect, a rather permanent strategic change in their companies, and in their approach to business. But we were also interested in specific changes in any of their extant policies or practices. In other words, had the economic downturn forced any changes in the way they actually conducted their business?

La Parola introduced a new product line, and while First Fruits and Terra Nuova both report making no changes, for Netuitive it was a significant time of change. Perhaps the most significant has already been mentioned—the strategic or tactical change away from large deals toward "beachheads." The business case for this approach is sound. It actually has resulted in more new customers, and from the customers perspective, it's a less risky decision because

---

8. From Survey 5, June 2009.

it's a smaller decision. It's easier for customers, as Netuitive says, to justify both financially and technically a "smaller implementation scope" that leads to "quicker successes." For Netuitive, these successes have already led to new "add-on" business from these customers. Another change they report is "showing goodwill." They delivered some services to a large client for no charge because the client had no cash to move ahead. But the client (ATT) was so impressed that they have recommended Netuitive to their own top competitor, and have upped their budgets for next year to spend more with Netuitive.

With respect to marketing, Netuitive has changed their focus to diversify, to market directly, and to leverage their customer base. In terms of diversification, banks now account for less than 50% of new customers. The direct marketing means more targeted approaches using one-on-one contact and telemarketing. In their words, there is "less brand/ego marketing and more personal/direct outreach and qualification of prospects." In an effort to leverage their customer base, Netuitive has created a customer forum where customers can interact with each other using blogs and online discussion groups and can interact with Netuitive's technology group, and can self-train. They have also revamped their travel policies, assigned a travel budget, granted no salary increases in 2009, and restructured executive bonuses to save cash. In research and development they have scaled back the number of projects, reorganized and rationalized the reporting structure ("which paradoxically led to better internal processes and communication") and they adopted an "agile development" approach in contrast to the old waterfall approach — which is essentially a change from top-down to collaborative. Netuitive also reports a strong focus on customer support (presumably this is a change) which led to 100% renewals of maintenance contracts. They report that this is exceptional in the industry.

Mundell & Associates has intensified their sales and marketing efforts at all staff levels by assigning small but measurable work to all staff that includes contacting existing clients, looking at new areas, and adjusting strategies. They are also investing in their website, launching a new logo, and have changed their Statement of Qualifications package to increase their competitive position. They have also increased their support of some initiatives in the local community that have been struggling. One example of this is a firm that teaches about animals and ecology to school children. When the schools cut back on their contracts, Mundell & Associates sponsored this firm to visit local schools, both Catholic and public, and believes the effort built sincere and significant goodwill in the community.

CHB reacted by increasing marketing mostly through referral programs and developing new accounts. The effort was partly successful, resulting in a slightly more diversified customer base. This was offset by the loss of several smaller clients which in turn led to refocusing on larger medium-size clients.

In part, the response to these challenges involved changed perspectives, particularly on the part of the company owner. The owner of Mundell & Associates realized he had personally grown attached to the relationships and experienced personal hurt, but at the same time was compelled to question the whole notion of employee turnover and its place in an EOC company. If one of the values is relationship—indeed if the guiding value is relationships, then what is the meaning and significance of employees wanting to leave? The answer revolves around the level of responsibility for someone's destiny. Relationships don't necessarily have to be permanent and unchanging, but there is room, perhaps even a necessity, for investing in a relationship for however long that relationship is privileged to exist. On a more practical level, at Mundell & Associates, this led to a more disciplined approach to performance reviews, and to providing employees with timely and useful feedback.

Netuitive points to a specific example of an interview for a sales rep position and a candidate actually offering to disclose confidential competitive information. Netuitive, as a way of testing this candidate, asked if he was willing to bring his customer database with him and share it because theoretically that information could have been very valuable to Netuitive. Once the candidate answered "yes," Netuitive decided not to hire him because that clearly violated their understanding of ethics and integrity. Why did they decide to do this? Because they had made a prior choice to build a values driven company, and that needs to be substanti-ated—that's their word—even when the company could benefit. But Netuitive goes on to say that they highlight the situations in order to teach and learn from them and to teach and learn with each other and to reinforce that their values are not just a poster that hangs on the wall near the entrance but that they are lived and tested every day. Netuitive also indicates that they believe that "These core values are good for the business in the long-run and we try to instill that belief in our colleagues by showing the fruits of certain be-havior. We do not want to reduce this to a utilitarian view of our values but to tell some employees that were asked to cut corners in their previous jobs that our values are appreci-ated here in good and bad times." The owner of Spiritours was forced to clarify the company's identity particularly in regard to issues of people who might be in controversial positions *vis a vis* the church, and it has also led to a reduced propensity to take risk.

There is one story we'd like to present verbatim since it is so illustrative. This is Netuitive's struggle with the 2008 economic downturn:

> The financial crisis impacted our business pretty hard as the large orders from large banks (our largest customer base)

evaporated in 2008. After trying every possible cost reduction measure such as salary freezes, cuts in bonus, marketing, and in travel, etc... we had come to the conclusion that the only way to save the company and to balance our budget was a reduction in force (30% of total). We had been very transparent about the economic situation of the company all along and had continuous discussions with employees and especially the wider management team (not just the execs but also all the managers throughout the company). The dreaded decision became inevitable in our eyes and we decided to make it a Netuitive moment, where we could put our best intentions and values at work. We involved each manager in defining the decision criteria/selection process on who to make redundant and every decision was truly a group decision. The most important discussion was on how we would treat the personnel made redundant. It became quickly apparent that most of the team wanted to do the right thing: put people first and make sure we did everything possible to help them out, both in terms of severance, in providing positive references and helping in the new job search. We unanimously agreed to size severances at the high end of the possible range, way above industry standards, even if it meant reducing the now-more-than-ever-precious cash on hand for the company. We wanted to put the people first. When I presented the plan to the board, it raised some eye-brows; I feel that they allowed us to go ahead with it because they saw how responsible we were being in trying to salvage the company. We also wanted to treat the employees with utmost dignity and make sure they understood that this was not a reflection on them as people but that it was a last-resort decision. The results exceeded our expectations. We announced the results in early August. The terminated employees did recognize the significant effort that the company made with the severances ("This is more than fair" was a dominant comment) and there were many scenes where they were consoling the remaining employees who were in tears. The minimum severance was one month for recent hires... To our joy, within one month each and every employee had found a new job (in the midst of the economic crisis). Another unexpected result is that many of those employees have provided many positive references for the company with customers and with new prospective employees as the economic conditions improved. This crisis ended up being a moment of truth. It truly cemented our team and its belief in our corporate values. In times of hardship, we were able to stick to our core principles and not throw them away in the name of economic imperatives (which could have been the perfect excuse to do so). Our employees have seen firsthand that doing the right thing not only makes one a better person and brings a lot of serenity and peace but can also pay off in the long term too. They experienced some of the fruits of providence in their lives.[9]

As we argued near the beginning of this chapter, EOC companies are not at all immune from the stresses and challenges of business life. And, as with all business owners, they have both identified some fairly routine responses, and some rather inventive responses to these challenges. A fair question to ask, then, was about guiding principles: on what do they rely when faced with the issues they have resolved?

Guiding Principles and Practice

All of these companies quickly point to the EOC values and Focolare mentality of "giving" versus just "taking" as providing guidance and stability when faced with any and all of these challenges. Many of the companies express EOC values in language as simple as the Golden Rule. For Finish Line the guiding principle is to "apply the Golden Rule and go with what's right." Variations on this approach also come from Sofia Violins and La Parola. Mundell & Associates strives to internalize EOC principles in the company culture, realizing that doing so can engender deeper respect for those principles among employees and begin

---

9. From Survey 10, December 2009

to create some sense of solidarity particularly when fellow employees, customers, or even competitors are dealing with difficult issues. Spiritours suggests that EOC values can provide solutions to current and future economic problems, such as the 2008 crisis. The fundamental EOC value that surfaces again and again with these companies in these defining moments is "placing the person at the center of the enterprise."[10]

One of the very interesting aspects of this value, articulated in just this way, is that for EOC business owners, this is a very concrete idea and expression. To others, including the researchers, this initially seems to be a very abstract notion. Let us provide an example. You'll recall that Netuitive narrated a long and complex retelling of the decision to reduce its workforce in response to the economic crisis. Later, after the downsizing was concluded and displaced employees had moved on, the CEO was able to reflect on that experience for the company, specifically as a concrete expression of this idea of people-centeredness. Note his use of the phrase "moment of truth," a clear identification of this episode as a defining moment in the life of the company and its people.

> *It was a real moment of truth as it was an opportunity to stick* to our corporate values and demonstrate to ourselves and to all employees that we were true to them. It helped crystallize the fact that our corporate values are part of our identity and not just feel/look-good statements. The way the difficult reorganization decisions have been made and executed — collaboratively and in the open, with large disclosure of the financials and the efforts we were making to

---

10. It is not clear whether this exact phrase appears in any official EOC literature, or is published in any way in any of the academic literature, but it certainly has been clearly and frequently voiced by almost every EOC business owner we have encountered. It infuses their conversation inside their companies and among each other. It comes about as close to an EOC mantra as anything else we have heard or observed. So, we produce it here as a direct quotation, although we have no source to cite.

help the terminated employees as much as possible; execs
making sacrifices first—has turned the existing and former
employees of Netuitive into even stronger supporters of the
company and our values. To the point of having terminated
employees act as references for possible new hires, now that
the situation appears to be improving. Existing and former
employees told us that we had been "exemplary," "more than
fair," "true to ourselves," "people-centered," "proud of the
company"... I feel that this crisis cemented the employees'
beliefs in our corporate values and helped them (in various
degrees) make them theirs. I also feel that many of them now
have a model to follow in times of crisis. It's not just about
the cold numbers, but putting the person first made us feel
that we were doing the right thing. We were proud of how
we managed through this crisis, no matter the outcome (We
could have gone bankrupt or been sold). The fact that sales
are up again and that we could have our best year ever now
looks like a providential sign...[11]

Accompanying this ethical compass however are some
recurring practices that serve these EOC business owners
on a continual basis, and that don't just surface when facing
a crisis. And, these practices go a long way toward providing constancy in their day-to-day business life. Foremost
among these is the frequent contact and collaboration
among these EOC business owners, certainly among those
in North America, but there is also a significant sharing
throughout the world. Our EOC business owners know each
other, and generally know each other well. They participate
in quarterly conference phone calls, but also can be, and are,
in much more frequent contact via e-mail and sometimes
Skype. While this interaction is certainly an opportunity to
discuss crucial business matters, it is also, and maybe more
importantly, an opportunity to simply share experiences of
participating in the EOC and to openly talk about seeing

---

11. From Survey 5, June 2009

the gospel incarnated in the world. One business executive (from Netuitive) talks about this association and fellowship reinforcing his belief system and his commitment to highly ethical standards. Further he sees it as a way to "reduce and hopefully one day eliminate the remnants of 'profit only' and 'political calculus'."[12]

This same executive also though makes the point that EOC values are not unique and extant only in the EOC, but rather are universal, which makes it possible to enjoy the benefit of working with like-minded colleagues even colleagues who may not share the EOC bond. And so discussion and consideration of values becomes part and parcel of company life and integral to decision-making at all levels. This too informs their ethical stance. Other business owners readily identify certain practices that shape their consideration of ethical matters—indeed most business matters—that are expressed in language probably unique to the EOC but are not necessarily unique practices in themselves. For example, the practice of "seeing things together" refers to resolving conflict through explicit and intentional consideration of the differing perspectives of everyone involved or affected by situations or decisions. A particular Focolare expression, "Jesus in the midst" has several meanings, but inside an EOC company it points to the recognition that no one in the company is ever alone, or faced with making decisions, alone, and is therefore an expression of considerable solidarity. Other business owners can readily identify the social doctrines of the Church,[13] their own value systems, their own spiritual reflection and prayer life.

When it comes to any formal written or otherwise articulated code of ethics or statement of principles, responses

---

12. From Field Study Interviews, April 2010.
13. This is most often referred to as Catholic Social Teaching; again of which there are innumerable sources and expressions. The Compendium is the most comprehensive source for further exploration. Pontifical Council for Justice and Peace. 2005. *Compendium of the Social Doctrine of the Church.* USCCB Communications.

are quite varied. Finish Line simply replies that each person understands they operate by the Golden Rule. First Fruits indicates for their rentals they have a code of ethics that's part of the association that they belong to. So it's really not theirs, and then for their farm and their rentals, they too go by the Golden Rule. Netuitive to this point indicates that they do explicitly list their core values and go through them with each new employee. It's a collection of principles rather than a formal policy. They really don't have a Human Resources department. Those are their words. They list their core values. They are integrity, honesty, meaning honesty and accountability, innovation that's customer focused, determination, passion and sense of urgency, teamwork marked by open communication, trust and respect, and fun celebrating success.

But Netuitive indicates that they try to explain these in the context of real-life situations, by providing examples, so that it's alive and it's not just a list of values. They do not speak about Trinitarian-like relationships even though the owner indicates that's his own benchmark, personal reference point for teamwork. But they look to translate these concepts into understandable language, and again, making them concrete. For example, sharing their experiences to show that there's a lot of depth behind each of the values that they talk about. Mundell & Associates indicates in response to this that they do not have it written down although they think that would be a good idea and a code would make sense. CHB in response to this just simply says, "As a solo-preneur I carry my code of ethics within me."

But for all this, there is no escaping the sentiment expressed by Spiritours; *I have always adhered to the principles and did my best to put them into practice; now I feel I must do more than my best, really live by those principles with God's grace and most importantly build relationships.*

I cannot live by those principles by myself; I need God's help and my peers' help."[14]

Summary Observations

These EOC businesses seem to pay attention—with equal measure and with equal seriousness—to the ideals of unity that motivate their formation of businesses and to the demands of the particular marketplace. There is *both an ideal and a practical ethos.* The EOC is an idealistic project;[15] that is to say, it is motivated by an ideal and yet it is a very practical project at the same time. What could be more practical than funneling business profits to those in need? This accounts for what is a refreshingly naïve, even somewhat off-putting, expectation that providence is at work, and that they are always willing and generally unwitting partners in that work. The ideal coexists with a straightforward can do, must do, practicality. They embrace the demands of the ideal, and yet also embrace the demands of the business. And, there appears to be no hand-wringing, no prolonged or protracted analysis, weighing of options or alternatives, and no parsing on any ethical fine points.

This combination provides what appears to us as *bias toward ethical action.* This appears to be the case whether the ethical situations they described for us were simple or complex; where simple might be a customer looking for a refund and complex might be dealing with fraud as in the case of Sofia Violins, or effecting a significant reduction in force requiring a termination in employment for employees as at Netuitive. It's almost as though there is no sense of "dilemma"—there's no distress at being confronted with a decision to make or a problem to be solved. In this sense they are quite grounded. They are not seeking perfection;

14. From Field Study Interviews, June 2010.
15. Molteni, Mario. 2002. "Development Problems in Businesses with 'Ideal Motivations,' in *The Economy of Communion: Toward a Multi-dimensional Economic Culture*, Luigino Bruni, (ed). Hyde Park: New City Press.

they know they cannot be perfect. But they also know that if they live the ideal, then God can perfect the work if he chooses. This doesn't mean they are at all removed from the torment, the human suffering, the pain, and the agony that can accompany life's decisions. They hurt and they struggle, and they learn, and they keep looking to live unity in the moment.

One cannot help but be encouraged and inspired by what these companies say about the reaction to economic troubles. The test of their principles and beliefs has strengthened their commitment. Perhaps this is truly courage at work; and, as so often happens in the presence of courage, others were inspired too. Frankly, if there is any area where we might think an EOC company would stand head and shoulders above the crowd in business, it would be in this area: in management sharing the pain with employees, in employees mindful of the common good, in preserving the dignity of all through prudent decision making and through perseverance and magnanimity. Faith in providence is also front and center in their thinking, a far cry from mere faith in the market.

Certainly the most prevalent question they ask when faced with challenges is about "the right thing to do." They tend to lead with that question rather than mechanically impose an answer. They really want to understand the matter. In their words, "Get to the core/spirit of the matter verses checking a box," and then they refer to their core principles. They believe in leading by example. Again, it's about being concrete and not abstract. They do have a systematic discussion with new employees and during annual reviews. But they also indicate that they have discussions when concrete situations arise, again, fleeing from the abstract, and again, reinforcing that these are creative moments. This is when they actually create the identity of their company. And they spend a lot of time recruiting and developing people so that the culture has meaning and can be perpetuated and can grow.

And, finally, what else is on display here in the manner we see EOC companies responding to challenges is their commitment to remaking the economic system. This is predicated on their understanding that every economic transaction is really a transaction between persons, and so it is never "just business, and not personal." Every act at work is understood as a means to live out beliefs. It should come as no surprise that EOC business owners describe the relationships with their own employees as the most significant business challenges they face. Given the primacy of relationships, employees are the innermost circle in the entire constellation of relationships that are created simply by virtue of being in business. These are the persons with whom one is in contact every day; with whom one is most closely associated; with whom one shares destiny.

Chapter Eight

EOC Companies:
Reflections and Conclusions

Some colleagues say they put a mask on when
they go to work and claim to be different
people at work than they are at home. This is
wrong. You cannot be happy like that. If you
aspire to be at peace with yourself or you are
trying to do what is right, and love your neigh-
bor, and build a relationship on reciprocity and
love, it becomes more and more difficult to be
in a system where you are pushed to do things
differently.[1]

This quotation is from the CEO of Netuitive and in many
ways it touches on perhaps the most fundamental observation we might make about Economy of Communion companies. Before we discuss it further, let us recap our journey
thus far. We began this volume with questions about the
precise nature of the EOC and some observations about
the complexity of that question. We argued also that any
answer to that question had to begin with an understanding
of the business practices of EOC companies. There were a
number of reasons for our argument. One is that companies
reveal themselves in their actions and behavior. Another is
that companies are what they do. These are not exactly the
same thing.

---

1. From Field Study Interviews, April 2010.

To say that companies reveal themselves in their actions and behaviors is to recognize that it is important to get past what companies may say about themselves and what they stand for, and to look at what they really do; to consider what their competitive behavior, their treatment of customers, and their regard for employees, say about what they believe and understand about themselves. To say that companies are what they do is to recognize an empirical fact about organizations and organizational life that has been observed by scholars for most of the last century or so, beginning, as we note, with Max Weber. Moreover, the process of institutionalization is part of our common experience; the process by which an organization develops and refines its values in response to its experiences, its crises, its celebrations, its failures and its triumphs.

And, whatever else it may be, the EOC is a special case. Whether we think of EOC companies as motivated by ideals, as social entrepreneurship, the project is accompanied by lofty language—a new style of economic action—and lofty ideals. So, whether we might be cynical or celebratory about the prospect of such an initiative, it still is important to ask ourselves how do these companies actually conduct their business. So, this is what we set out to do—to describe the business practices of the EOC to the extent that we were able to uncover them. Our objective was not to judge them, not to hold them up as a model, not to dismiss them as impractical, not to look to catch them in some sort of hypocrisy, not to compare them to other companies, not to compare them in any way to a set of best practices, but simply to describe.

Let's review then what we've been able to identify as particular business practices; and we'll do so pretty much in chapter order. In terms of marketing practices, these companies demonstrate a habit of listening and responding to customers, but also listening to their own insight, intuition and experience. There is very little formal market research that takes place (with Netuitive being a notable exception) but substantive evidence of a habitual sensitivity to the needs and wants of customers. Notably, almost all of these companies occupy a singular, if not unique, market niche that is a bit challenging to explain. This gives many of them a stout, if not sustainable, competitive advantage; in fact it makes them quite valuable to their customers, and mitigates direct competition at the same time. Mundell & Associates has specialized expertise, Netuitive and Sofia Violins occupy quite specialized niche markets, Spiritours offers the retreat aspect—the silence, the walking pilgrimages—and Terra Nuova offers a unique restoration service. Spiritours seems to have a particular "openness to opportunity." For example, the development of the trip to Santiago de Compostela seemed to grow out of both the owner's intuition and the intuition of a friend. The safari in Kenya was also opportunistic, as well as the Sahara desert retreat. Finish Line seems to embody the principle of focusing on customers and not on competitors. The challenge is deciphering the extent to which the advantages of uniqueness with all its attendant benefits create some space for them to pursue the EOC ideals.

One can hardly overstate the central position of word of mouth, reputation and relationship marketing in these EOC companies. It is one thing they all have in common and something in which they all take pride. It's interesting that having a well-crafted message to deliver is not equally important. Perhaps the power of word of mouth is not about details—pricing, quality of work, capability, flexibility and turnaround—as it is about trust and appeal to the character of people and the organization itself. Word of mouth, though obviously effective, also poses significant risks. One bad experience, one verbal and aggressively unhappy customer could potentially do a lot of harm. It also appears that the companies rely more and more on web technologies to get their message out. Several have all but given up on brochures.

The companies vary significantly in their use of communications methods for marketing and promotion. None appears to have a marketing person whose work is dedicated to this cause, nor does there seem to be a pattern of approaches. However, the businesses do tend to sort themselves out on a continuum from the simplest of approaches (business cards and letterhead) to the more complex (websites and YouTube videos). The larger companies, of course, are the ones who make the most use of the various communication technologies and who also seem to have a good grasp of the need for a strong, clear message. It's interesting that the companies, in general, are quite modest in staking their claims as EOC businesses. Mundell & Associates and Spiritours go farthest here. But, surprisingly, some of the companies make no mention of EOC at all.

In general, each of these companies demonstrates a keen awareness of their identity as EOC companies and unquestionably the commitment to the EOC ideal is paramount, and this plays a role in their approaches to marketing although it is often quite understated. Spiritours is quite explicit in offering a product whose unique value is connected with "EOC" values and philosophy. The concern for customers in the delivery of services that Finish Line and La Parola expressed also have obvious connections, but not as strong as Spiritours. Dealerflow also talks to some extent about a product that facilitates unity in the corporate environment. On the whole the owners described their products in clear and concise terms, but the level of detail differs significantly among them. La Parola is very informal, almost intuitive. One might wonder if this is really a business or a ministry. Netuitive and Mundell & Associates, on the other hand, offered significant technical descriptions of their services and seemed well-tuned into the idea of a special value proposition.

The response from Spiritours regarding the marketing message is interesting. The company has made an effort to tailor their promotional material to attract different audiences. This approach has succeeded in bringing in people who are genuinely looking for one of the special trip options Spiritours is offering. But, a skeptic might wonder about people for whom spirituality is instrumental; that is just one dimension of the "good life." The Spiritours message would resonate with them as well as genuine seekers. But any company that puts out any kind of message can only speak from the heart—speak from their center. And, maybe it's not a bad thing to attract people for whom spirituality is currently instrumental—maybe a few weeks on a Spiritours tour will be life-changing. And therein lays a certain tension that is perhaps intrinsic to all of these companies and their business practices.

With respect to competitive behavior, clearly the guiding principle for these companies is their view of their business as a set of relationships, and this has a significant effect on the approaches to competition. Certainly we noted what we've described as an unwavering and uncompromising commitment to reliability of both products and services and this too fosters a particular approach to competition. It's fair to describe these companies as more customer focused then competitor focused. This appears to carry over into their approaches to pricing. Most of these companies take a purely "cost-based" approach to pricing that is not in any apparent way geared or pegged to competitors.

When it comes to investment in their operations, EOC owners tend to be risk averse, being careful to spend or invest only what cash flow the business generates, although Netuitive was certainly an exception to that at start-up and Mundell now carefully manages a substantial line of credit. Nevertheless, what is apparent is a certain brand of fiscal conservatism, and a concern for the use of resources that rises to the level of admirable stewardship. Perhaps this conservatism explains the emphasis on careful planning, goal setting, and the measurement of progress. At the same time, there is an obvious reliance on intuition and perhaps this is not unusual for entrepreneurs; they rely on their own sense about how well or not so well they are doing. They go to great lengths to prepare themselves for the unexpected and to feel they are flexible, fluid, and responsive. And finally, they demonstrate again the importance to them of relationships in their attitudes toward both suppliers and employees where attitudes of dependence, participation, and teamwork prevail. It is clearly important to these business owners to find ways to help employees develop; to grow and become the persons they seek to be.

Hiring practices are grounded in an awareness of "hiring for community" that pervades both their hiring criteria and their hiring processes. This is certainly in line with their sense of identity as EOC companies, although surprisingly there is considerable variability of employee orientation and disclosure (explanation) of the EOC mission. In some ways, the most interesting information about hiring practices in the EOC companies is what is not there. There is virtually no language about hiring to mission, or about prospective employees' attitudes about God or any particular faith. Anyone who looks at the EOC and worries that the businesses might be parochial because the shared mission is rooted in the Christian tradition will be reassured on this point. Not that reassurance is important to us, but it does seem that in terms of hiring, these businesses look very much like other businesses, even on the "God" questions. Perhaps it is a testament to the owners' sincerity in focusing on the whole person not on the person's faith, religion or lack of either. Or to their commitment to unity, which cannot be limited to the few, the chosen, or "people like us." It is possible—and this is not a question we probed with the owners—that the quiet is due to concerns about driving people away. One owner hinted at this possibility, it seems, in reference to having "more courage to speak" about EOC to part-time employees than to address the question openly with her staff.

As for knowledge, skills, experience and attitudes, their expectations seem to fit the nature of the individual businesses, both as to particular skills and to the business's size and complexity. To point out that there is a range of planning for hiring and variation in the clarity of process for hiring seems a bit obvious; naturally different companies have different practices. Again, it's not surprising to note that the larger companies (in terms of employees) use more extensive and regularized methods than the smaller ones. One or two of the companies seem to be acting at or near a level of generic best practices in their hiring practices. How they compare to competitors we do not know. What does come across strongly among the businesses that hire are concerns for the impact of a hire on the "team," a term that is, we believe, more a proxy for "community" than for "competitive unit." How will this person fit into our team? What will this person add to our team? Involving "the team" in interviews and related language suggests that the businesses do not take an individualistic approach in their hiring, i.e., getting the optimal candidate from the perspective of professional qualifications. Rather, the concern is for both qualifications and the person as a member of the work community.

These companies appear to share similar cultural aspects marked by openness and mutual respect, and they appear to take the development of culture seriously and intentionally. This too is in keeping with their sense of identity and with EOC values and is perhaps where the EOC emphasis on the business as a community or a set of relationships is most visible. Clearly, they strive to be familial and embrace storytelling and celebrations for example, and do not generally embrace formal mission and vision statements. (Mundell & Associates and Finish Line are notable exceptions). The

salient characteristic here might simply be a tendency toward informality. Generally speaking, the leaders of these
EOC companies demonstrate a preference for action; they
are doers first and talkers later. Clearly this is tied to the
EOC ideal to live first the spirituality of unity, but we would
argue that it also demonstrates a keen awareness of the necessity for leaders to "walk the talk."

On one hand, the companies and their leaders demonstrate considerable flexibility, responsiveness, and willingness to change, both in the product and service arena but
also in matters of internal practice and policy. But again
that flexibility is grounded in their understanding of the
business as community. And, it is that same grounding that
also drives them to stand their ground in other ways. As we
noted in our chapter on defining moments:

We find EOC companies walking away from business opportunities, scrupulously following regulations,
cheerfully (sometimes reluctantly) refunding payments,
participating in the civic process while avoiding attempts at
undue influence, making restitution where appropriate, and
looking to reconcile with detractors.

We noted also a pervasive confidence in meeting challenges head-on with a preference for ethical action. As
leaders, these business owners don't appear to suffer a
great deal of angst about challenges, ethical or otherwise,
but rather appear more committed to doing the right thing
in the moment than to a set of grand overarching policies.
Their approach to risk-taking is fairly eclectic, but on the
whole probably best described as rather conservative. And
in the arena of profit distribution, there exists some openness about the use of profits, but otherwise we noted a very
top-down, owner-centered and directed decision-making
approach. For that matter, we can also point to a fairly
unsophisticated understanding of profit. For most of these
business-owners, the sense of profit is very accounting
oriented (e.g., considered on a post-tax basis only). Many

of these companies provide support funding and services to their local communities in ways that reduce their bottom line. But this is not generally viewed as "profit sharing" or a profit reduction technique. In fact, in our chapter on culture and leadership we questioned the breadth and depth of strategic imagination that might be the foundation for more ambitious growth plans. It's difficult to imagine any of the EOC businesses harboring plans for significant growth or market penetration (e.g., by acquisition), that might in the long run generate greater and more sustainable profits.

We said at the beginning of this volume, and several times since, that our task was to produce a description of EOC company business practices without comparison or judgment. But we also noted near the beginning that quite a bit of our own interest and we suspect the interest of others in the EOC is precisely with questions of both comparison and judgment. In particular, we believe there is widespread hope, largely unspoken, that business people can be better citizens and at the same time, widespread cynicism that businesses have little choice but to be ruthless competitors. In fact, our early discussion about isomorphism suggests that such cynicism might be well founded. The pressures of competitive capitalist markets have not lessened since Weber's characterized them as an iron cage.

Our response to that has been to think hypothetically; that is, had we resolved to begin this study with a set of testable hypotheses, what might those be?

If we ask ourselves what we might "find" or "learn" from our research, one possibility might be that there are no business practices among our EOC companies that distinguish them in any way from non-EOC companies.

Or, we might find that some of their business practices are indeed different. If some of their business practices are different, of course we would be able to describe which ones, and explain how they are different.

And, if some of their business practices are different, are they the same practices among the EOC companies? In other words, do all the EOC companies differ from non-EOC companies in, say, advertising? Or, are the differences more random?

Also, if some of their business practices are different, are the EOC practices similar enough to each other to be labeled an "EOC way" in particular practices?

Finally, are there a sufficient number of practices among EOC companies that distinguish them from non-EOC companies, AND that are similar enough to each other to allow us to speculate that there might be an EOC way of doing business?

In partial answer we can certainly say that there is no evidence that general employment practices distinguish EOC companies from others, but there is some evidence of patterns and unique practices. These might include employee participation in hiring, an emphasis on organizational/personal "fit," an emphasis on working in teams and the impact of new team members. There exists little language about hiring to mission, or about faith, or God, or the EOC. These companies vary in complexity, sophistication and use of business practices; they demonstrate a range of performance in regard to "best practices," and owners certainly use the language and philosophy of EOC to express ideas and describe practices. Generally, restraint and modesty prevails, which leads us to question whether the power of the EOC ideal has been fully unleashed.

All of which brings us finally to address the title of this volume. What, indeed, do we mean by "structures of grace"?

First and foremost, the title reflects our conviction that EOC companies are indeed different. And that difference is centered on a conviction of the business as a set of relationships, or more accurately, a *community,* and the conviction that the purpose of economic activity—the production and distribution of goods and services—is to bring people together, to create *community*. For us, this is the defining characteristic of the EOC. These companies embody the process described by Selznick as institutionalization:

> The test of infusion with value is expendability. If an organization is merely an instrument, it will be readily altered or cast aside when a more efficient tool becomes available. Most organizations are thus expendable. When value-infusion takes place, however, there is a resistance to change. People feel a sense of personal loss; the "identity" of the group or community seems somehow to be violated; they bow to economic or technological considerations only reluctantly, with regret....
>
> From the standpoint of social systems rather than persons, organizations become infused with value as they come to symbolize the community's aspirations, its sense of identity. Some organizations perform this function more readily and fully than others. An organization that does take on this symbolic meaning has some claim on the community to avoid liquidation or transformation on purely technical or economic grounds.[2]

EOC companies are a concrete realization of our aspirations and our identity. They pass the expendability test, and they do lay claim on our society to not bow down to economic expediency. Thus, where Weber argued that organizations would all become the same strictly due to economic pressures *vis a vis* the competitive capitalist markets, and later scholars particularly argued that organizations would all become the same due to legitimacy concerns, Selznick opens a door to the idea that an organization can resist these. Indeed resist these is not exactly correct. Organizations infused with value become less susceptible to these pressures and become invested with meaning for a community,

---

2. Selznick, pp 18 and 19.

as symbols of aspiration and an expression of identity. They might become in this sense an organization of hope.

Moreover, to return to the passage from Netuitive that opened this chapter, they provide an answer to the modern dilemma of the divided life.[3] They also provide an example of what has been called a "structure of virtue."[4] With our title, we want to simply raise the question whether EOC companies might go slightly beyond a structure of virtue, where business leaders look to create business practices that facilitate the inculcation of virtues. Might the EOC ideal of community raise the possibility that business practices aimed—not at economic efficiency or social legitimacy, or even inculcation of virtue, but—at unity become a means of grace?

The notion of structures of virtue or in our case structures of grace is a response to the insistence of John Paul II on the existence of "structures of sin." As human beings, we create institutions and social structures: governments, local governments, town governments, homeowners' associations, colleges, universities, corporations, small businesses, large businesses, and non-profit agencies. These institutions and social structures shape us: they shape our behavior, they shape our values, they shape our thinking, they shape our aspirations; they shape our choices; they shape our sense of right and wrong. They shape what we believe to be true. They shape our entire understanding of reality. They shape our understanding of God, of salvation.

Oftentimes we have created a social structure that really takes us down the wrong path. We need to think about how nihilistic our culture is, and how widely accepted certain interpretations of reality are, and how difficult it is to raise

---

3. There is a large and substantive body of literature here from many disciplines that raise or address this phenomenon. Let us cite the recent publication of the Pontifical Council for Justice and Peace; *Vocation of the Business Leader; A Reflection.*

4. Again, this is a idea rapidly gaining currency. We first encountered it in Alford, Helen, O.P., Clark, Charles, M.A., Cortright, S.A., Naughton, Michael, J. 2006. *Rediscovering Abundance*. South Bend:, IN:. University of Notre Dame Press, p 31.

children while depending on the culture's structures — the school system and all of it — to shape them in ways that we would like to see them shaped. And when we become part of a company, an employee, we almost unwittingly, because of their ways of doing things, get caught up in ways of doing things that really are not good, that in fact lead to sin.

If in fact we can create social structures that promote or reward, in many cases, acting in our self-interest, that reward acting in sinful ways, that condone sinful ways, is it not possible to create social structures that would foster something different? Can we not create social structures that would foster community, that would foster a culture of life, that would work against the prevailing structures and promote the best in human behavior and not the worst? And, when God joins with the work of human hands, it must be possible to create social structures that foster sanctity. It's not our work, it's not our doing that sanctifies, but it's our doing, our structures that create the opportunity. So is it possible for human beings to create structures that are sanctifying, and that, in effect, contribute to making us holy? If it's possible for us to cooperate with God's grace, the answer must be yes. And what might such structures look like? They might look like Economy of Communion companies.

Appendix

Research Methodology

W hen we began this project in 2008, we had already completed a case study of one EOC company, Mundell & Associates, Inc. At that time there were fewer than 50 EOC companies in North America, all of them privately owned. Little information about them was therefore publicly available. Thanks to introductions initiated by the founder of Mundell, 14 of those companies accepted our invitation to participate in this project. Two were Canadian and the rest were U.S. companies. The companies themselves and their products and services are described in Chapter One. We had three overall goals for the project: first, to describe accurately how the EOC businesses operated; second, to describe their practices in the larger context of business practices today; and third, to look for distinguishing characteristics among the companies' practices that might be suggestive of an "EOC identity."

Research Design

An immediate challenge before us was to plan a method for gathering data that would be flexible enough to accommodate the differences among the businesses involved and honor the time constraints of owners who already had their hands full in leading what were basically entrepreneurial, and in most cases, startup enterprises. Though we needed to be systematic, i.e., asking the same questions of each business, we also needed to be able to probe answers, if necessary, to seek clarification. We needed a research design that would accommodate the dynamic interactions between researcher and principal which is typical of original case research. To achieve these ends, we planned to use several rounds of inquiry and with each round "cast a net" in a specific direction, e.g., toward financial practices or communications with customers, and follow up with respondents by telephone, e-mail, and even in person, if possible. Through this process we would accumulate relevant data on the actual business practices of the companies in our study and perhaps learn about the thinking behind these practices. Then we would examine data among the companies in search of patterns, anomalies and unique examples, and finally develop a narrative that described their business practices and shed light on the thinking behind them.[1]

Data Collection

When we invited principals to participate in the study we explained our purposes, methodology, and intended output and explained that as participants they would be responding to a series of questionnaires with approximately 10 open-ended questions each, to be distributed monthly. Respondents were asked to return completed surveys within three weeks. We promised confidentiality in reporting actual sales, costs, margins, profits and salaries. Each questionnaire contained an identical statement of consent and confidentiality. Believing that some participants might still be concerned about how we handled sensitive information, we agreed to honor requests to opt out of particular questions.

What started as a ten-month time frame stretched into eighteen months—November 2008 to May 2010. Turnaround times for some questionnaires were longer than expected, particularly in 2009, during the financial crisis. Already burdened owners found they had less time than planned to complete our surveys. On our end we needed

---

1. The several data gather approaches (surveys, focus groups, interviews, site visits) and analytical approaches we used are consistent with the multi-method evidence gathering in case study research. See, for example, Yin, Robert K. 2014. *Case Study Research: Design and Methods.* Los Angeles: Sage Publications.

extra time to prompt respondents who had not returned surveys, to take stock of the data we were getting, to ask for more information from some respondents, to decide what further probing could be included in a later survey and so on. Multiple interactions with participants supplemented the survey instruments; including occasional telephone interviews, e-mail communications and some in-person interviews. Data gathering also included site visits to seven of the 14 businesses in the study. Also during those 18 months, August 2009 to be exact, we led a two-part focus group with eight of the participating owners at an annual meeting of the North American EOC timed to coincide with distribution of a survey on decision making practices around profit distribution.

In all, a series of 12 survey questionnaires went out, each focusing on a single aspect of business function or activity, with questions designed to elicit objective and subjective data on the subject of the questionnaire. Survey titles signaled their content. Wherever possible, we asked respondents to provide examples or stories to explain their answers and occasionally we requested documents that would provide more complete explanations. The open-ended style of most questions invited respondents to answer using their own terms and explanations, and to highlight their concerns and reasons for approaching functions or activities as they did. In this way we hoped to invite them to tell us in their own words how a business that "puts the person at the center of the enterprise" and practices a "spirituality of unity" might approach that activity. So each of the 12 questionnaires served at least two purposes; one, reporting data relevant to a particular function or activity, and two, reporting on the thinking and values upon which the company's choices rested. A full list and description of each survey is contained in the following table:

Survey No.	Title	Description	Date
1	Business Overview	Basic data about the company; official name, organizational structure, product descriptions, location, revenues, employees.	November 2008
2	Employee Hiring Practices	Solicited stories about prior hires and sought data on hiring practices.	December 2008
3	Marketing Research, Pricing, and Sales	Solicited stories about pricing decisions, and sought data about product development, and sales cycles.	February 2009
4	Marketing Communications and Promotion	Sought data about advertising and promotion practices and about modes of disseminating information.	April 2009
5	Managing in a Recessionary Economy	Solicited narrative about the effects of the 2008 recession on the business and on management practices and decisions.	June 2009
6	Profits and Profit Distribution Decisions	A hybrid questionnaire accompanied by focus group sessions; sought data on profit distribution decisions.	August 2009
7	Finance – Funding Sources	Sought data about starting the business particularly sources of funding, advice, and counsel.	September 2009

8	Finance – Funding Sources	Sought data about operating and maintaining the business after startup with particular attention to financing.	October 2009
9	Operations	Sought data about work flow, capital deployment, human resources, development, and training practices.	November 2009
10	Business Challenges	Solicited stories about prior significant business challenges and then responses to those challenges.	December 2009
11	Organizational Culture	Solicited stories and sought data about shared experiences, and about intentional practices aimed at building culture.	February 2010
12	Ethics	Sought stories of ethical dilemmas faced and resolved, and specific ethical attitudes and practices.	May 2010

Data Analysis

As the surveys were returned, we read them carefully, checking for completeness, looking first for indications that the questions had been fully understood and noting where a respondent had volunteered information not related directly to the questions asked, but interesting anyway. A little past the halfway point in distribution of the 12 surveys, we began a more systematic study of data already in hand, focusing on 1) collaborative review and reflection; 2) synthesis of the data; 3) a search for patterns, anomalies and consistency in practice. The typical steps in data analysis and interpretation went something like this. First, we each read the complete set of responses to a questionnaire, then agreed on our assignments of questions for more in depth review, e.g., one of us would take the even numbered items and the other would get the odd. As we each read our assigned items more thoroughly, we made notes about factual observations, questions and insights. Then, in a phone conversation dedicated to that questionnaire we moved through it item by item, first one of us taking the lead, then the other, as we worked our way through all the data. What points stood out? What had individual owners said—or failed to say—that was noteworthy? What similarities or differences in practice stood out? Was there evidence of patterns in practices? And finally, what general impressions or conclusions did we take away, or what new questions did the data raise? Time and again we were challenged in this process to *describe* business practices. When we thought we saw a pattern or commonality in practices, we had to think carefully about whether they were enough alike to be grouped together. What "label" could we use that would hold the group without suggesting evaluation or inviting comparison? After these phone conversations we typed up and exchanged summaries of what we had said to be used for ongoing review and reflection, particularly when we got to the writing stage.

Because the surveys spanned 18 months and at least a dozen management topics, we tried not to be biased about *where* information appeared or *when* it reached us. This approach proved fortuitous because through it we developed the habit of looking across surveys as well as within them to get a complete picture of business practices in our sample companies. This allowed us to combine information from sources disparate (in content) and distant (in time) into passages and/or chapters that combined material in categories that did more than mirror the survey topics.

Limitations

In addition to the limitations present in any qualitative study and in case research in general, we recognize the problems with this study arise from inconsistent and partial survey responses, drop outs, and the longitudinal nature of our survey approach. Participants varied in the amount of information they provided and in the consistency with which they provided it but in our view, full participation was very strong. All 12 completed surveys were returned by eight of the 12 participating companies, 10 and 9 each by two others, but in each of these cases owners provided the relevant information during site visits. One respondent returned just four surveys and another three. Early in the survey process we realized that questions might have serious relevance for some companies but little for others, and this seemed to be related primarily to the size and maturity of the business. Eight of the principals responding to our surveys were able to participate in a focus group session. Site visits were made at seven of the companies. Two of the fourteen companies that agreed to participate in the study initially did not participate at all.

We acknowledge that there was nothing random in the companies selected to participate in this study. On the contrary, they all participated as EOC member businesses precisely because they *are* EOC businesses. We can only surmise that their generosity in staying the course over so many months and in investing countless hours of their time in this study suggests a sincere desire to learn more about themselves and fellow EOC participants and, of course, to share their experience with others.

References

Aggravating Circumstances: A Status Report on Rudeness in America. Pew Charitable Trust. Public Agenda. 2001. (http://www.publica-genda.org/files/pdf/aggravating_circumstances.pdf)

Alford, Helen, O.P., Clark, Charles, M.A., Cortright, S.A., Naughton, Michael, J. 2006. *Rediscovering Abundance.* Indiana. University of Notre Dame Press.

Anthony, William P., Kacmar, K. Michele, Perrewé, Pamela L. 2010. *Human Resource Management: A Strategic Approach.* USA: Cengage Learning.

Armstrong, Gary and Kotler, Philip. 2008. *Marketing: An Introduction.* 9e. Prentice Hall.

Badaracco, Joseph L., Jr. 1997. *Defining Moments: When Managers Must Choose between Right and Right.* Boston, MA. Harvard Business School Press.

Besanko, David; Dranove, David; Shanley, Mark; and Schaeffer, Scott. 2003. *Economics of Strategy,* 3e. USA. Wiley, John & Sons, Incorporated.

Bolman, Lee G., and Deal, Terrence E., 2008. *Reframing Organizations: Artistry, Choice and Leadership.* San Francisco, CA. Jossey-Bass.

Bruni, Luigino. 2002. *The Economy of Communion: Toward a Multi-Dimensional Economic Culture.* New York, New City Press.

Collins, Jim. 2001. *Good to Great.* New York. HarperCollins Publishers.

Collins, Jim and Porras, Jerry I. 2004. *Built to Last: Successful Habits of Visionary Companies* HarperBusiness. USA.

Deal, Terrence E., and Kennedy, Allan A. 1982. *Corporate Cultures: The Rites and Rituals of Corporate Life.* USA. Addison-Wesley.

DiMaggio, P.J. and Powell, W.W. 1983. "The Iron Cage Revisited: Institutional Isomorphism and Collective Rationality in Organizational Fields". *American Sociological Review,* Vol. 48, No. 2.

Drucker, Peter. 1974. *Management; Tasks, Responsibilities, and Practices.* New York. Harper & Row.

Drucker, Peter F. 2001. *The Essential Drucker: Selections from the Management Works of Peter F. Drucker.* New York. HarperBusiness. HarperCollins Publishers.

Ferrucci, Alberto. 2002. "A Different Economic Dimension: The Experience of the Economy of Communion." *The Economy of Communion: Toward a Multi-Dimensional Economic Culture.* New York, New City Press.

Gallagher, Jim. 1997. *Chiara Lubich: A Woman's Work: The Story of the Focolare Movement and its Founder.* New York. New City Press.

Ghemawat, Pankaj. 2011. *World 3.0.* USA. HBSP.

Gold, Lorna. 2002. Conference of the WCC/WLF/WARC/CEC/RvK. *Economy in the Service of Life,* Amersfoort 18th June.

Gold, Lorna. 2010. *New Financial Horizons: The Emergence of an Economy of Communion.* New York, New City Press.

Greenleaf, Robert. 1977. *Servant Leadership: A Journey in to the Nature of Legitimate Power & Greatness.* New York, Paulist Press.

Halberstam, David. 1986. *The Reckoning.* New York. William Morrow & Co. (HarperCollins).

Hammer, Michael and Champy, James, 1993. *Reengineering the Corporation: A Manifesto for Business Revolution.* New York, HarperCollins.

Heizer, Jay, and Render, Barry. 2010. *Operations Management.* 10th edition. New Jersey, Prentice Hall.

King, W.R. and Cleland D.I. 1979, *Strategic Planning and Policy.* New York. Van Nostrand Reinhold.

Levitt, Theodore. 1975 "Marketing Myopia", *Harvard Business Review.* MA. HBSP.

Lubich, Chiara. 1999. "The Experience of the Economy of Communion: A Proposal for Economic Action from the Spirituality of Unity", presented at the Strasbourg Conference of Political Movements for Unity. May 1999.

Lubich, Chiara.2006. *Essential Writings.* Michael Vandeleene, ed. New York: New City Press.

Meyer, J.W., and Rowan, B. 1977. Institutionalized Organizations: Formal structure as myth and ceremony. American Journal of Sociology, 83: 357.

Molteni, Mario. 2002. "Development Problems in Businesses with 'Ideal Motivations'. in *The Economy of Communion: Toward a Multi-dimensional Economic Culture*, Luigino Bruni, (ed). New York. New City Press.

Perrow, Charles. 1986. *Complex Organizations: A Critical Essay*. McGraw-Hill. New York. 3e.

Peters, Tom, and Waterman, Robert H, Jr., 1982. *In Search of Excellence*. USA. Harper & Row.

Pontifical Council for Justice and Peace. 2005. *Compendium of the Social Doctrine of the Church*. USCCB Communications.

Pontifical Council for Justice and Peace. 2012. *Vocation of the Business Leader: A Reflection*. USCCB Communications.

Rarick, Charles and Vitton, John. 1995. "Mission Statements Make Cents," *Journal of Business Strategy*, 16.

Ratzinger, Cardinal Joseph. 2004. *Introduction to Christianity*. San Francisco: Ignatius Press.

Sager, Ira and Burrows, Peter. 1998, "Back to the Future at Apple". *BusinessWeek*. May 25.

Schein, Edgar. 1992. *Organizational Culture and Leadership*. San Francisco, CA. Jossey-Bass Inc.

Schor, Juliet. 2004. *Born to Buy: The Commercialized Child and the New Consumer Culture*. Scribners, NY.

Scott, W. Richard. 1981. *Organizations: Rational, Natural, and Open Systems*. Prentice Hall. Englewood Cliffs, New Jersey. 3e.

Selznick, Philip. 1957. *Leadership in Administration*. New York: Harper & Row.

Tirole, Jean. 1988. The Theory of Industrial Organization. USA. MIT Press.

von Hippel, Eric. 1994. *The Sources of Innovation*, USA. Oxford University Press.

Weber, Max. 1968. *Economy and Society: An Outline of Interpretive Sociology*. New York: Bedminster.

Yellin, Emily, 2009. *Your Call is (Not That) Important to Us: Customer Service and What It Reveals About Our World and Our Lives*. New York. Free Press.

Yin, Robert K. 1984. *Case Study Research: Design and Methods*. Sage Publications. California.

Index

Administrative behavior, 16

Advertising, 51–52, 56
  word-of-mouth, 51

Aggravating Circumstances: A Status Report on Rudeness in America (Pew Charitable Trust), 41, n42

American Express, 143

Anthony, William P.; Kacmar, K. Michele; and Perrewé, Pamela L., n112

Arc-en-Saisons
  company profile, 26, 33–34
  culture, 141
  defining moments, 163
  EOC connection,
    communication of, 131
  hiring, 118, 131
    orientation, 131
  legal structure, 33–34
  marketing,
    promotion, 61
    research, 45
  pricing, 79, 81–83
  principal, about the, 33
  planning, 96
  product development, 47
  promotion, 61
  responding to challenges, 164
  startup, 33–34
  tax issues, 163
  teamwork, 104
  values, 164

Archdiocese of Montreal, 54

Armstrong, Gary and Kotler, Philip, 78n

Badaracco, Joseph L., n155, 156, 157

Besanko, David; Dranove, David; Shanley, Mark and Schaeffer, Scott, n77

Bolman, Lee G. and Deal, Terrence E., 136, 137

Bootstrapping, 88

Branding, 56

Bruni, Luigino, 19, 87

Built to Last: Successful Habits of Visionary Companies (Collins and Porras), 143

Business, as a community, 23, 111, 185, 188–189
  nature of, 66

Business Network International (BNI), 55

Business Week, 41

Catholic Social Teaching, 174

Challenges, responding to, 164

CHB Associates, LLC
  company profile, 26, 36
  culture, 141
  EOC connection,
    communicating, 60
  defining moments, 159, 164

economic downturn, impact
  of, 159, 168
ethics, 175
legal structure, 36
marketing, 44, 55, 60–61
relationships, 55
research, 44
web, 61
performance measures,
  relationships as key to
    success, 67, 96
pricing, 79, 81
principal, about the, 33
products, 47
relationship marketing, 55
responding to challenges,
  164
responsiveness, 96
sales cycle, 73
startup, 36, 89
values, 146

Coercive forces in shaping
  organizations, 18

Collaboration as competitive
  differentiation, 69

Collins, Jim, n109

Collins, Jim and Porras, Jerry,
  143

Communion
  as the true objective of
    business activity, 21, 97,
    111
  of goods, 21, 23

Communities of work
  qualities of, 97, 111

Company profiles, 26,

Competition
  competitive awareness, 65,
    70

**Consort International (dba
  Sofia Violins), 27**

*Corporate Cultures: The Rites
  and Rituals of Corporate Life*
  (Deal and Kennedy), 136

Crosby, Philip, 68

Culture, 69, 135–141
  artifacts, 138–140, 154
  celebrations, 146
  collaboration, 69
  customer understanding of,
    141
  of giving, 20, 148–149, 151
  spreading, 24
  leadership role in shaping,
    138–139, 147
  uniformity of, 139
  values, 137–140, 189

Customers, 42–43

Deal, Terrence E. and
  Kennedy, Allen A., 136

Dealerflow Corporation
  company profile, 26, 33
  EOC connection,
    communicating, 131
  employees, 115–116
    development and training,
      129–130
  financing operations, 130
  hiring practices, 115–116,
    120, 124
    orientation, 129–130,
  legal structure, 33
  marketing, 45–46
    research, 45–46
  principal, about the, 33
  sales cycle, 72
  startup, 33

teamwork, 130

Decision-making, 150–152, 186

Decoupling in organizations (DiMaggio and Powell) 18

Defining moments, 155–157
  with collaborators, 159, 162
  with customers, 159
  due to competition, 159
  in economic downturn, 158, 166
  intellectual property rights, 159
  lawsuit, 163
  relationships,
    employee, 161, 163
    collaborator, 166
    customer, 64
  taxation, 163–164
  theft, 162

Deming, W. Edwards, 68

Development Dimensions International and Electronic Recruiting Exchange, n113

DiMaggio and Powell, 18n, 66n

Disney, 143

Divided life, x, 190

Drucker, Peter F., n39, 40, 42

Economic downturn, impact of, 158
  responding to, 165–168
  strategic impact of, 166–168

Economy of Communion (EOC)
  audits of business activity by, 149

business as a community, 23, 185, 188–189
in Canada, 31, 33
culture,
  of giving, 20, 24, 148–149, 151
  described, 13, 87, 140–141
  uniformity among businesses, 139–140
  artifacts of, 154
  storytelling, 142–143
defining, 13–15, 20, 23, 141
distribution of profits, three part, 21
executive compensation, 149
expression of "spirituality of unity," 13
ethical principles, 171–174
faith connections, 13
founding in Sao Paulo in 1991, 20
in Freedom, 21, 149
governance, 24
history, 19–20
humanizing the economy, 14
ideals, 14
  development of business, 22, 23
International Commission, 24
  assessing needs of Focolare, 24
  and spreading the culture of giving, 24–25
management requirements and style, 23–24
marketing in, 57, 62, 181
  EOC affiliation, 57–59, 61
  experience in, 45
  listening as, 43
  niche, 47, 62, 181
  relationship, 62

reputation, 62
word-of-mouth, 51, 62, 181
marketing communications,
65, 181–182
membership requirements,
87
mission statements in EOC
companies, 144
North American businesses
as research subjects, 26
owners, interaction among,
173
participants, 21–22
philosophy, 14–15,
prophetic component of, 25
pragmatic generosity, as
EOC value, 153
principles, general, 22–23
profits, sharing with those
in need, 24
and culture of giving,
148–149, 151
providence, relying on, 142,
153, 177
roots in Focolare, 13
storytelling, 142
values, 25, 145–146, 171–
172
worldwide, 21–22

*The Economy of Communion:
Toward a Multi-Dimensional
Economic Culture* (Bruni),
19, 87.

eoc Finish Line
company profile, 26, 31–32
culture, 141, 142
EOC connection,
communicating, 131
defining moments, 160–162
economic downturn, impact
of, 166
employees, 104

development and training,
130
orientation, 130
profiles, 98–99
ethics, 174
financing operations, 32
hiring,
practices, 99–100, 117, 120,
124
as strategic activity, 117, 120
legal structure, 32
marketing,
promotion, 52, 55, 57–58
relationship, 55
research, 44, 181
web, 57–58
performance measures,
92–93
quality as key, 67–68
relationships as key, 67, 96
pricing, 79
principal, about the, 31–32
planning, 91, 96
product, 31, 47, 79
development, 47
profits, distribution of, 150
relationships, importance,
67
reputation, importance of,
120
responsiveness, 94
sales cycle, 79
startup, 31
success measures,
relationships as key, 67
quality as key, 67–68
values, 146, 171

*Economy and Society: An
Outline of Interpretive
Sociology* (Weber), 18

Efficiency, logic of (Weber), 16

EMA, 44

Employee development, 97,
102–104

Employee ownership, 103–
104

Equipment, financing, 87–89

Employee ownership (ESOP),
162

Ethics,
codes of ethics, 175–176
standards, 173–174

Financing, at startup, 87–88,
183
bootstrapping, 88

First Fruits Farm
company profile, 26, 35
culture, 141
EOC connection,
communicating, 131
defining moments, 160, 162
economic downturn, impact
of, 166
employees,
development and training,
130
orientation, 13
profiles, 119
ethics, 175
financing operations, 89
hiring practices, 119–123
legal structure, 35
marketing,
promotion, 58
research, 44
performance measures,
relationships as key, 67, 98
pricing, 80–81
principal, about the 35
profits, distribution of, 151
planning, 96

product development, 47
relationships,
as key to success, 67
supplier, 92
sales cycle, 72
startup, 35
values, 146

Focolare
assessing needs of, 24
beliefs, 20, 139, 145, 171
culture of giving, 20
EOC roots in, 19
founding in Trent, Italy, 20
governance, structure of, 24
Lubich, Chiara, founder, 20,
111
spirituality of unity, 16, 20
values, 139, 145

Ford, 143

Forrester, 44

Fortune 100 companies, 44

Freedom, individual vs.
institutional constraints,
128

Gallagher, Jim, n20

Gartner, 44

General Electric, 143

Generosity, pragmatic
decisions about, 153

Gift of self, as Focolare value,
145

Gold, Lorna, n22, n97

Golden Rule, 67, 124, 171

Great Crisis of 2008, n158

Greenleaf, Robert, n86, 109

Hammer, Michael, 68

Hammer, Michael and
    Champy, James, n85

Heizer, Jay and Render, Barry,
    n90, 94

Hiring, 98, 110, 184
    for with community, 111,
        116–117
    job descriptions, 98
    key characteristics sought,
        121–122
    knowledge, skills and
        attitudes in, 185, 117–
        120
    processes, 23, 113–114,
        116, 123–127
        design of, 123
    serendipity in, 116, 126
    as strategic activity, 110–
        114, 117, 120–121

Homogenization (DiMaggio
    and Powell), 18

Humanizing the economy, 14

IBM, 143

**Ideal Safety Communications,
    Inc.**
    company profile, 26, 32–33
    employee profiles, 131
    hiring practices, 100, 119,
        123, 131
    legal structure, 32
    marketing research, 44
    performance measures,
        relationships as key, 96
    pricing, 81
    principal, about the, 32
    planning, 96
    sales cycle, 72

Ideals, EOC, 22–24

Institutionalization, dynamics
    of (Selznick), 16–17, 156,
    164

International Commission of
    EOC, 24

Iron cage (Weber), 18

Isomorphism (Meyers and
    Rowan), 18

"Jesus in the midst," 174

Jobs, Steve, n43

John Paul II, 190

Johnson & Johnson, 128

Juran, Joseph M., 68

King, W. R. and Cleland, D. I.,
    n144

Knowledge, skills, and
    attitudes (KSA's), 117

La Parola
    company profile, 26, 35–36
    culture, 142
    economic downturn, impact
        of, 159, 166
    hiring practices, 98, 100
    legal structure, 36
    marketing research, 43–44
    performance measures,
        relationships as key, 67, 96
    planning, 90, 96
    principal, about the 35–36
    product development, 47
    profits, distribution of, 151
    relationships as key to
        success, 68

responding to challenges, 164
responsiveness, 94
sales cycle, 71
startup, 35–36
values, 146, 182

Leadership, 17, 139, 147–152

Leadership and Administration (Selznick), 16, 110, 189

Legitimacy (Meyer and Rowan), 18

Levitt, Theodore, n40

Logic of efficiency, 16

Lubich, Chiara, 20, 111n

Luthiers, 118

Management: Tasks, Responsibilities, Practices (Drucker), n39, 40

Marketing, 57, 62, 181
communications, 65, 181–182
experience in, 45
listening as, 43
niche, 45, 62, 181
relationship, 62
reputation, 62
research, 43, 45
word-of-mouth, 51, 62, 181

Marketing oriented companies, 40

McDonalds, 128

Medtronic, 128

Merck, 143

Methodology, of EOC study, 7–11, 193–199

data analysis, 197–198
data collection, 194–195
limitations, 199
research design, 193
subjects, 26
surveys, 196–197

Meyer, J. W. and Rowan, B., 18n

Mimetic forces in shaping organizations (Meyer and Rowan), 18

Mission statements, 143–144, 185

Molteni, Mario, n176

Mundell & Associates, Inc.
company profile, 26, 28–29
culture, 69, 141–145, 152
EOC connection,
communicating, 59, 61–62, 130
decision-making, participation in, 99
defining moments, 159–161, 164, 168
economic downturn, impact of, 166, 168
employees,
development and training, 100, 103, 129
orientation, 129–130
ownership (ESOP), 103
profiles, 98, 121
turnover, 161
ethics, 175
financing operations, 88
hiring practices, 98–99, 121, 124–126
as strategic activity, 117, 121
internships, 152
job descriptions, 98, 100–101

legal structure, 29
marketing,
    communications, 52, 55
    relationship, 55
    research, 45
    strategy, 58–59, 181
    web, 59, 63
mission, 144–145
organization chart, 79, 100
performance measures, 92
    relationships as key, 93
    quality as key, 68
pricing, 79–80
principal, about the, 28
planning, 91, 96
products, 19
    product development, 49
profits, distribution of, 152
relationships,
    as key to success,
        reputation, 52, 58
responding to challenges,
    161
responsiveness, 94–95
sales,
    cycle, 71
    practices, 74–75
startup, 88
teamwork, 104
values, 66, 129, 182, 126,
    146

National Public Radio (NPR),
    55

Netuitive, Inc.
company profile, 26, 25–27
culture, 69, 141, 146
EOC connection,
    communicating, 66,
        130–131
defining moments, 159–
    161, 172–173

economic downturn, impact
    of, 158–159
employees, 27
    development and training,
        101, 103
    orientation, 128–129
    ownership (ESOP), 103
    participation, 105
    profiles, 98, 101, 120
    turnover, 102
ethics, 175–176
financing operations, 88–89
hiring practices, 98, 101,
    169, 120–127,
    interviewing, 127, 169
    leadership, 103
job descriptions, 98, 101
legal structure, 25–27
marketing, 27, 53
    communications,
    promotion, 52, 56
    relationship building, 53
    research 44, 181
    strategy, 53
mission, 127
organization chart, 98–99
ownership, employee, 103
performance measures, 92
    relationships as key,
    quality as key, 67
pricing, 79–80
principal, about the, 25
planning, 91, 96, 167
products, 47, 49
product development, 49
relationships,
    as key to success, 53
    supplier, 92–93
responding to challenges,
    169–171
responsiveness, 95–96
sales cycle, 72–73
startup, 25, 88
strategy, 27, 69, 167

values, 98, 127, 146, 172, 175

Nimbleness, 94–96

Organizational Culture and Leadership (Schein), 136

Organizational life, tension of, 24

Organizations, creation of, 16

Orientation, new employee, 128
at Arc-en-Saisons, 131

Participation, 104–106

Performance measures, 91–92

Person at the center of the enterprise, 76, 172–173
people-centered organization, 145

Perrow, Charles, n16, 156

Peters, Thomas J. and Waterman, Robert H., n40, 41

Pew Charitable Trust, 41

Planning, 89–91

Pontifical Council for Justice and Peace, n190

Present moment, living, 70

Pricing
cost-based, 77, 81
cost-value relationship, 81–82
discrimination, 77
implications for business practices 75
psychology of 77
value-based, 77, 81

Pricing practices, 79–81

Process design, 96

Proctor & Gamble, 128, 143

Product development, 46–47

Production-oriented companies, 40

Professional Business Coach Alliance, 44

Profits,
Distribution of, 147–150, 186–187
three-part distribution of, 21, 149–152
"sending money to Rome," 24

Promotion, 50–51, 61

Providence, reliance on, 142, 153, 177
role of in success, 65, 75

Quality (defining), 68–70
Gestalt of, 69–70
as unwavering and uncompromised reliability, 68

Quality circles, 68

Rarick, Charles and Viton, John, n144

Reengineering the Corporation: A Manifesto for Business Revolution (Hammer and Champy), 85

Reframing Organizations: Artistry, Choice and Leadership (Bolman and Deal), 136, 137

Relationships, 62, 181
  as competitive advantage,
    66, 82
  as key to success, 66–67,
    145
  as a moral choice, 82
  stressed in advertising,
    communications, 51–52

Reputation, 52, 62, 181
  stressed in advertising,
    communication, 51–52

Risk (risk-taking), 183, 186

Rudeness in America, 41–42

Sales practices and selling,
  71–74
  Sales cycles, 71

Schein, Edgar, n126, 137, 138,
  139, 147

Schor, Juliet, n51

In Search of Excellence (Peters
  and Waterman), 40, 41

Seeing things together, 24,
  174

Sending money to Rome, 24

Selznick, Philip, 16, 110, 156,
  63, 189

Six sigma, 68

Solidarity, 171

Solopreneur, 86

Sophia University, 20

**Sophia Violin, Consort
  International dba**
  company profile, 26, 27–28
  culture, 142

EOC connection,
  communicating, 60
defining moments, 162, 165
economic downturn, impact
  of, 159,165
employees, 28
  ownership (ESOP), 162
  profiles, 102, 118–119
  training and development,
    102–103
  turnover, 102
ethics, 176
financing, startup and
  operations, 27–28, 88
hiring practices, 102,
  118–119, 123
leadership, 102
legal structure, 28
luthiers, 118
marketing, 59–60
  brand, 60
  research, 44
performance measures,
  relationships as key, 67
  quality as key, 68
pricing, 81
principal, about the, 27–28
planning, 96, 118
products, 27–28
  product development, 49
relationships,
  as key to success, 67
  supplier, 91, 118
responsiveness, 94
sales cycle, 72–74
startup, 88

Spiritours
company profile, 26, 28–29
culture, 141–142
EOC connection,
  communicating, 63,
    130–132

decision-making, 104
  participative, 114
defining moments, 114–
  115, 159, 163
economic downturn, impact
  of, 166
employees,
  development and training,
    129
  orientation, 129
  ownership (ESOP),
  profiles, 100, 120
ethics, 175
financing operations,
hiring, importance of, 117
  interviews, 125, 131–132
  practices, 100, 114–116,
    120, 122, 124–125, 142
legal structure, 30–31
marketing,
  communications, 54
  message, 56–57, 183
  promotion, 52, 55
  research, 44, 181
  web, 57
mission, 125
pricing, 79
principal, about the, 29–30
planning, 79, 96
products, 29–30
  development, 48–49
profits, distribution of, 150
relationships,
as key to success, 67, 114
sales, cycle, 72–74
  practices, 74
startup, 30–31
success measures,
  relationships as key, 67
  quality as key, 68
teamwork, 104
values, 125, 146

Spirituality of unity, 16, 51,
  165

Starbucks, 128
Statistical process control
  (SPC), 68
Structures,
  of companies, 34
  of grace, 23, 188–191
  of sin, 190
  of virtue, 190
Success, 65–68
  Golden Rule as key to, 67
  as set of relationships,
    66–67, 70, 183
  as quality product or
    service, 67–68
Sustainability, 66

Teams, 97, 104–105, 130, 185
Terra Nuova Restorations
  company profile, 26, 34–35
  customers, culture and, 141
  economic downturn, impact
    of, 159, 166
  financing operations, 89
  legal structure, 34
  marketing, 44
    communications, 52, 61
    relationships in, 54–55
    reputation, 54
    research, 44
    web, 61, 63
  planning, 90
  principal, about the, 34–35
  product development, 47
  sales cycle, 71
  startup, 89
Transparency, 141, 146
Trust, 54, 62, 145

Values,
  in culture, 137–140, 145–
    146, 189
  EOC, 25, 145–146
  Focolare, 145
  role in institutionalization
    (Selznick), 17

Weber, Max, 17, 18, 180, 187,
  189

Web marketing, 60

Work environment, 93–96

Workflow, defined, 90
  business process design, 86
  financial investment in, 87
  planning, 89–91
  and people, 96

Works of charity
  as Focolare value, 145

World Youth Day, 54

Yellin, Emily, 42

Yin, Robert K., n194

Young, Lew, 41, n42

*Your Call is (Not That)
  Important to Us* (Yellin), 42

NEW CITY PRESS
of the Focolare
Hyde Park, New York

New City Press is one of more than 20 publishing houses sponsored by the Focolare, a movement founded by Chiara Lubich to help bring about the realization of Jesus' prayer: "That all may be one" (John 17:21). In view of that goal, New City Press publishes books and resources that enrich the lives of people and help all to strive toward the unity of the entire human family. We are a member of the Association of Catholic Publishers.

Further Reading

Economy of Communion	978-1-56548-178-7	$11.95
New Financial Horizons	978-1-56548-354-5	$16.95
Wound and the Blessing	978-1-56548-428-3	$16.95
Leading Like Francis	978-1-56548-575-4	$14.95
5 Steps to Effective Student Leadership	978-1-56548-509-9	$4.95

Periodicals
Living City Magazine,
www.livingcitymagazine.com

Scan to join our mailing list for discounts and promotions

or go to

www.newcitypress.com

and click on "join our email list."